The Daring Daughters of Nantucket Island

How Island Women from the Seventeenth through the Nineteenth Centuries Lived a Life Contrary to Other American Women

Jascin Nolan Leonardo Finger

Jack's Shack Press

Nantucket, Mass.

2014

DEDICATION

For my parents, Jack and Melodee, who have given me the stars.

Contents

Acknowledgements i

But a Woman: An Introduction 1

Part One Daring Daughters: An Analysis of the Development of the
Woman's Sphere, Quakerism, and the Island of Nantucket in the
Seventeenth and Eighteenth Centuries 8

    The Colonial American Woman 9

    Nantucket Island 13

    Quakerism 17

    Quakerism on Nantucket Island 21

    Independent and Autonomous: Nantucket and Its Pioneer Women 30

Part Two "A Practical, Forceful Type of Woman:" Nantucket Women in
the Age of Woman's Sphere 42

    The Nineteenth Century and Woman's Sphere 44

    Maritime Communities 49

    Quaker Influences 55

    Nantucket Island 59

    Separation and Independence Breed Surprises and Secrets 67

    Women at Work on Nantucket 71

Conclusion: Beyond the Shores of Nantucket 83

Appendices 88

Notes 116

References 123

Index 136

"Standing under the canopy of the stars you can scarcely do a petty deed or think a wicked thought."

     – Maria Mitchell (1818-1889)

  I am who I am and know what I know, because of many truly amazing "stars" whom I have been blessed to know and to have as a part of my life, however briefly. They shine over me, guide me, and protect me, and their light is within me. I could not possibly list everyone who has shaped me and who is now and forever always will be a part of me. I am truly lucky to have such a wonderful family and friends and mentors. I have grown up surrounded by strong, intelligent, and independent women who have set an example for me, just as Nantucket's women of the nineteenth century and earlier stood as examples for other Nantucket women and women of the nation and the world. My Nana and Other Nana – Gloria Nolan Hartigan and Helen Fike Nolan – are two women who are a source of inspiration for me. Another source of inspiration is my great-grandmother, Beatrice "Mama Minnie" Leonardo, who came from Italy at the age of fourteen and married, giving birth to the first of her six children by the age of fifteen.

The women whom I have studied in the course of this research are also an inspiration to me and serve as mentors from the past. I thank them for the stories and diaries they left behind, but most of all for their independence and their belief that they could do whatever they set their minds to – Maria Mitchell, Lucretia Coffin Mott, Lydia Coleman Mitchell, Reverend Phebe Coffin Hanaford, Avis Pinkham, Abby Betts, Eliza Riddell, Nancy Hussey, Elizabeth Chase, Hannah Fosdick, Sarah Hiller, Sarah and Mary P. Swain, Anna Gardner, Reverend Louise Southard Baker, and so many, many more.

For the women – and men – of the Maria Mitchell Association –

my colleagues and mentors both past and present, I am eternally grateful. Kitty Pochman, Susan Beegel, Susan Laity, Laura Evans, Edith Andrews, Jane Stroup, Mimi Beman, Barb Maple, Clarissa Porter, Happy Shipley, Barbara Vigneau, Elizabeth Yager – all left an impression upon me as a teenager and as a young woman, and many have seen me into my adult years, still serving as my mentors. Those who have left us still continue on as mentors, as they are a part of me. I would like to thank my friend and mentor Linda Zola. I would also like to acknowledge the Maria Mitchell Association and its Board of Managers for providing me with the opportunity to work on a reduced schedule in the off-season so that I might pursue my master's degree. Additionally, I thank Janet Schulte and Ronnie Elwell for their support of and enthusiasm for my work. The Nantucket Historical Association and its Research Library staff are always helpful, in particular Marie "Ralph" Henke and Elizabeth "Libby" Oldham, appearing with information that they think might fit what I am investigating. Libby was also my editor for the exhibition that I created and curated for the Egan Maritime Foundation in 2007. That exhibition started me off in the direction of this topic, and I thank the Foundation for realizing that there were other Nantucket women who needed to be included, allowing me to expand the subject matter of the exhibition beyond just Maria Mitchell, who, I believe, would have wanted it that way. I had the wonderful advice and guidance of three fantastic and inspiring women as I worked on my masters' thesis that became this book. My advisory team for my Master of Arts degree in history consisted of Marion Nesbit, Ph.D. (Lesley University); Mary Dockray-Miller, Ph.D. (Lesley University); and Karen V. Hansen, Ph.D. (Brandeis University). What an honor to work with these talented and intelligent women who all rallied around my work and had positive comments and enthusiasm for my research – thank you! And I would like to thank Suzanne Gardner, editor extraordinaire, for reviewing this before publishing.

And finally, I need to thank and acknowledge my family – my "team" in all aspects of life. I list them all as number one. My parents and best friends, Jack and Melodee Leonardo, have always been there for me, in good and bad, with support, a shoulder to lean on, advice, the ability to listen and be patient, and always seeing that there is a roof over our heads. They have given me so many gifts, including the love and appreciation for history and its many facets, historic architecture, the art of being observant, a wonderful education in and out of the classroom, Nantucket, and the MMA. They have instilled in me my respect for others, for all living creatures, and for the world around us. They have created a strong and a so very close and loving family and serve as examples of what every person should be. I love you and thank you! I thank my brother, Jarrod, for being my friend and always being there for me – even if it's just a phone call to see how I am and to tell me a funny "Lisey story." I thank him too for adding such a loving and wonderful sister-in-law to our family and for bringing my wonderful niece and nephew into the world. Elise and Holden, I hope that you find inspiration in our family members and their stories. I will tell you many stories as you grow, since I believe that the more we tell their stories, the more we learn, and the more they continue to live as their names are spoken. Our son, Nolan Absalom, came along as I was wrapping this up. I hope Nolan that someday you appreciate the rich history of where we live and the amazing people who have made our family our family. Finally, I would like to thank my husband, my best friend, who once said to me, "I married you *and* the Mitchell House." Always a supporter of what I do, you are my cheerleader, the person who sends me back to the computer to work while taking over all of our household chores in addition to your own work so that I might research, learn, and write. Thank you for always being there for me and always supporting me. I love you more than you will ever realize.

Three unidentified Nantucket Girls, unknown date. P654a. *Photograph
courtesy of the Nantucket Historical Association.*

The Daring Daughters of Nantucket Island:
How Island Women from the Seventeenth
through the Nineteenth Century Lived a Life
Contrary to Other American Women

But a Woman: An Introduction

"For women there are undoubtedly great difficulties in the path, but so much the more to overcome. First, no woman should say, "I am but a woman." But a woman! What more can you ask to be. Born a woman, born with the average brain of humanity, born with more than the average heart, if you are mortal what higher destiny could you have. No matter where you are nor what you are, you are a power. Your influence is incalculable."

– Maria Mitchell (1818 – 1889)

Maria Mitchell was one of Nantucket Island's most illustrious daughters. America's first female astronomer and the first female professor of astronomy, Maria Mitchell was also the first woman and first American to win a gold medal from the King of Denmark for her discovery of a telescopic comet from Nantucket in 1847. The tiny island on which she grew up boasted a unique community and an even more extraordinary group of women. Nantucket's daughters were not "but women;" they were the backbone of the island and kept the community afloat. Maria Mitchell is a strong representative of the Nantucket women who came before her and served as a beacon for those who followed. She is one of the many shining female stars of a small island with an unusual story.

Despite modern transportation, Nantucket Island – located approximately thirty miles off the coast of Cape Cod, Massachusetts – was, and still is, an isolated and windswept spit of sand. The island has charmed, beguiled, and called to generations of people. It is not just surrounded by water; it is surrounded by dangerous shoals that have claimed the lives of thousands of mariners and everyday people. The "faraway island" and "grey lady," as it is often referred to, are monikers that are appropriate and telling. Often shrouded in fog and swept by gales, its grey-shingled and simple Quaker-styled homes present a dull, drab aura. When the sun shines, the purity of the sunlight, the intensity of the blue skies, and the green of the sea brighten the landscape. This quality of light is unmatched and enlivens a person.

Because of its solitude and beauty, as well as its interesting history, the island has long influenced authors and artists, from Herman Melville and John Steinbeck to Eastman Johnson and Elizabeth Rebecca Coffin. It has intrigued historians throughout time because of its unique place on the American and world stages. This tiny and remote island has played a role not only in American history but also in world history. Nantucket whalemen were known throughout the world for their prowess with the harpoon and their adventurous spirit. Historians as early as Hector St. John de Crèvecoeur (1735 – 1813) were recounting the history of the island and the unique people who inhabited it, including the island's women.

Nantucket women left an indelible mark on Crèvecoeur and continue to leave their mark on the island even today. The island, so unchanged by time, feels as if one might bump into Mrs. Hussey on her way down Main Street to open her shop on Centre Street, or that one might see children streaming into the Coffin School as the school day begins or Maria Mitchell on her way to the Atheneum to open the library for its patrons.

The women of Nantucket – particularly those living during the high point of the whalefishery on the island – were faced with a unique set of circumstances that allowed them freedoms that women elsewhere did not find to the degree that Nantucket women did. Faced with years alone while their husbands were whaling, Nantucket women were confronted with a sink or swim environment. They became the family leaders and, in many cases, the chief breadwinners, while their husbands were away at sea. On numerous occasions, men were lost at sea, while sometimes whaleships returned with a pitiful amount of whale oil in the cargo hold, leaving a family with a small income after three to five years of work. Nantucket women worked from within the home; many opened shops and set up businesses or other enterprises in order to earn money to provide for their families' needs. These women hired other Nantucket women.

A unique set of circumstances allowed these women to work and supported their endeavors, and it is these circumstances that are of interest and have offered enlightening investigations. The themes of religion, frontier, isolation, and a whaling-based economy shaped my investigations. The place of women in American society, and in particular the place of Quaker women, is still a subject that is greatly under-researched. In April 1987, a conference was held at the Quaker-founded Haverford College. Seven female scholars of women's history and Quaker history came together to present "Witnesses for Change: Quaker Women 1650 – 1987." This conference revealed that information concerning Quaker women and the influence they had on others and their independence had yet to be fully investigated. Twenty-seven years afterwards, this belief unfortunately still holds true. While some scholars have looked at Nantucket women and, indeed, the Quaker influence on the island, they have not necessarily looked at the influence Quakers had over their non-Quaker neighbors. In the case of Nantucket Island, they have not investigated in-depth the influence of whaling and Quakerism combined, nor taken into account the frontier qualities of the island. Nantucket women were faced with several factors that promoted their freedoms and independence of self and mind.

I undertook this research to discover something new about the roots of the strength and independence of Nantucket women. Like the authors and artists mentioned above, I too have been greatly influenced and beguiled by Nantucket Island – the place, its people, and its unique history. I first came to Nantucket just before my second year and celebrated that birthday on the island in a tiny cottage near Brant Point with my parents, my grandmother, and my great-grandmother – the latter two were women of force themselves, both strong and independent, who took on roles in their lifetimes that were not seen as the norm. No one at the time, least of all myself, realized what a love affair I would come to have with the island that I now call home. This love was instilled in me by my parents and has grown throughout my life, leading me to my current occupation on the island.

From the age of twelve, I became immersed in an island organization, the Nantucket Maria Mitchell Association. America's first female astronomer, Maria Mitchell, was a leader among women – and men – and inspired many generations of women to follow their dreams, no matter where they led them – even if it was into a "man's world." To that end, her students, friends, and family members began the MMA in her honor to perpetuate her legacy and preserve the house in which she was born. Since an early age, my education and plans for working adulthood were guided by this house, this woman, this organization, and this small island. Like Maria Mitchell and other Nantucket women, I grew up in an open-minded family that never saw gender, religious, or racial differences or looked askance at women in charge of family businesses or finances. My grandmother was a single parent and the sole breadwinner, raising my mother in the post-war era when the ideal of American society was a happy family, led by a father just home from the war. The men in my family supported their female partners; they differed from the "typical" American male who dominated the household. They did not see male versus female roles – they cooked, sewed, gardened and took on many tasks that even today are viewed as "woman's work."

When I was a young teenager, my friends on Nantucket consisted of women in their fifties through their nineties – women who were strong and independent women. These women were the essence of the MMA – they were its presidents, its department heads, and the friends, leaders, and members of the board and its committees. The founders of the MMA were mainly women, and these women were the ones who raised the funds and developed the governing documents of the organization. Many of the original founders were Nantucket women – women who had grown up in an environment in which women had many more powers than women elsewhere in the world. The women of the MMA in the 1980s were descendants of these founders, their friends, their students. As a young and impressionable twelve year old, I was surrounded by women who were my friends and mentors – whether they or I realized it at the time or not. Each one of them shaped me in some way and continues to live on inside me – they helped to make me who I am today – and Maria Mitchell, the MMA, the Mitchell House, and a small island have helped to shape me just as my family has.

My first, deeper study of the opportunities for Nantucket women came in 2007, when I researched, designed, and mounted an exhibition honoring Maria Mitchell and other Nantucket women for a collaboration between the MMA and the Egan Maritime Foundation (now Institute) titled "Gutsy Gals: From Hearth to Heavens, Maria Mitchell and Her Sister Nantucketers." With this exhibition, I finally was able to begin to research the history of Nantucket's unique female population. But I only scratched the surface and reluctantly had to close the books in order to begin my writing and planning of the exhibition, all the while hoping that at some point I could return to re-open the doors and shed more light on these remarkable women. My opportunity to re-open books, diaries, letters, and journals written by Nantucket women resulted in this book before you.

This book is presented in two parts – the seventeenth and eighteenth centuries and the nineteenth century when the status of women in America began to change in a more extreme manner. Adding further to the discussion, biographies of particular women or situations are presented. For the most part, these biographies have been placed into the body of the text in italics. More extensive biographies can be found in the appendices, along with images of some of the women studied.

The themes of religion, place, frontier, and economy are discussed throughout the work both in relationship to Nantucket and, to a lesser extent, the rest of America. In particular, a look at the idea behind Nantucket as a frontier place is closely examined – a theme heretofore overlooked by scholars and historians and which presents another reason why Nantucket women wielded power and enjoyed a fairly independent lifestyle.

In order to place Nantucket in context for a discussion of how Nantucket women and their situation were unique, a discussion is made concerning the place of American women in the colonial era when most lived on a frontier and worked towards a common goal – survival. Nantucket's differences from the mainland during this period are highlighted, including how the island was settled and the ways it differed from mainland communities. Once the setting is established, the history and tenets of the Quaker religion are addressed. The establishment of the Quaker religion on Nantucket is discussed, as well as how this compared to and contrasted with Quakerism elsewhere at the time, and the unique circumstances that allowed Quakerism to flourish on the island. The final portion of the discussion of the seventeenth and eighteenth centuries includes a look at several island women as entrepreneurs and their success despite, or, perhaps, because of the manner in which Nantucket continued to maintain its isolation and autonomy and, thus, its continuing status as a frontier.

In the second half, the place of women in nineteenth-century America is presented, with a focus on the roles of women in maritime communities, including some Quaker communities. The Quaker and whaling economy's influences on Nantucket are outlined. And finally, a closer look at Nantucket women – of all walks of life – in the nineteenth century is explored to determine what nineteenth-century island women did, why they did it, how their community supported their actions, and how they influenced women elsewhere in America.

Eliza G. Coffin made a statement that reflected words similar to those of Maria Mitchell's. In the May 9, 1874 issue of the local paper, Nantucket's *Inquirer and Mirror*, Coffin stated,

> Many entertain the idea that Woman's Sphere is
> confined to a certain limit, and any step beyond
> it is improper and greatly detracting from the true
> standard of womanhood. I believe that Woman's
> Sphere is every where (sic.), and her influence unlimited.
> (*Inquirer and Mirror*, May 9, 1874)

Coffin, Mitchell, and many island women – and men – from historians to artists to scientists and other luminaries and professionals, have noted throughout many generations and hundreds of years that Nantucket's daughters held a place not just in Nantucket society, but also in American society, as notable leaders who were independent, well-educated, and intelligent and who played an equal role on the national and world stages alongside Nantucket's and the nation's sons.

6

Part One – Daring Daughters: An Analysis of the Development of the Woman's Sphere, Quakerism, and the Island of Nantucket in the Seventeenth and Eighteenth Centuries

"The woman who does her work better than ever women did before, helps all womankind, not only now, but in all the future – she moves the whole race no matter if it is only a differential movement – it is growth."

– Maria Mitchell (1818 – 1889)

Early colonial New England was a place of religious and political freedom, opportunity, adventure, and new beginnings. For governing bodies, it meant an expansion of empire, new raw materials, and, in some instances, ridding the home country of undesirable citizens, typically religious upstarts and the poor. Colonial New England was a frontier, where women and men worked together for the survival of their families, with a focus on the homestead and what the family produced; everyone worked towards a common goal. By the end of the eighteenth century, as towns and cities developed and the frontier disappeared from New England, families were no longer focused on working together for their subsistence in the same way, unless they were farming families. By the late eighteenth century, men and boys were beginning to work outside the home and the idea that the family worked together with everyone sharing similar work tasks changed. The public sphere was left to men, with most women tending exclusively to their families and domestic chores. With the development of industrialization, what women had produced and what had served as a major contribution to the family's survival was now a product of a market-oriented economy; goods could now be produced in bulk by manufactories and purchased from local shopkeepers and stores. While not all families could make such purchases and women continued to produce at home as before, the ideal was to be a consumer of goods produced by others.

Families were now in need of cash to purchase goods, and males were tasked with making this happen. In rural areas, where communities and economies continued to be underdeveloped, this was not necessarily possible and this caused the American economy and the position of people in society to develop unevenly from one place to another. The separation of the family, and thus the sexes, which was caused by the growing market economy, was further reinforced by religion, law, and even popular publications such as magazines and ladies' journals. However, there was at least one place that did not follow this trend. Remote Nantucket Island remained a frontier throughout the eighteenth century. This independent community continued to foster the life of a frontier throughout the eighteenth and into the nineteenth centuries, supported in part by the Quaker religion, whaling, and the pragmatism necessary for living in isolation. These characteristics allowed Nantucket women to continue to play an active and important role in the family and in community economies.

The Colonial American Woman

The Colonial American Woman and the Corporate Family Economy

In the colonial American period, the household was the center of life, society, and the small, primitive American economy. As scholar Mary Ryan notes, an interdependence, necessary for survival, existed among the family members. This "corporate family economy," as she calls it, was "a domestic system of production that bound family members together, as a single body, in the common enterprise of subsistence"[1] and was found on the frontier.

The frontier was fleeting. As a place developed and its economy grew, a frontier no longer existed in that place, because the town or small city was better connected to other communities and the population no longer had to rely almost exclusively on one another for survival. The close-knit community and mentality of working together for survival dissipated – it was not as basic an instinct as it once was. The frontier swept across America as expansion pushed from east to west. The frontier was a place of survival and of families working together within a community to ensure the community's viability at its basic level – the survival of each and every member to ensure that the community succeeded. While the frontier and the life found on it did leave as a place developed, frontier conditions continued to exist in the United States well into the late nineteenth and early twentieth centuries. Pockets of frontier life could be found throughout the country and, in these places, economic development took a long time in arriving and taking hold.

While the male was the head of the household, both women and men worked together for the survival of their family. There was some division of labor based on sex, according to Ryan[2]; however, women were able to easily "transgress against the economic authority of the male household,"[3] and "if their husbands were artisans or shopkeepers, women managed the family business whenever necessary."[4] Scholar Sara Evans notes that women played an important role in village life as they traded goods with one another that they had produced at home, using these products towards their family's subsistence.[5] Even in small cities, women were expert at trading goods with one another, relying heavily, more so than farm women did, on this trade, "yet their households retained the undifferentiated quality of more rural farmhouses."[6] The goal was the survival of the family, and all women, no matter where they were living, rolled up their sleeves and contributed, active in the process of subsistence and not simply relying on the male head of the household. Many women engaged in physical labor, including toiling in the fields alongside their husbands, and this work was accomplished in addition to their domestic chores of tending to home and numerous children. However, they were not just preparing meals or looking after the children within the home, they were creating the items necessary for family use and for use in the trade that they conducted. Items produced in the home by women, such as candles, soap, butter, spun wool, and woven cloth, all meant that a family could both take care of itself and trade these items for products they did not make themselves. Again, survival was the key and women were active players in assuring the family's survival within the small, primitive economy of the colonial period.

The trade of household-manufactured goods conducted between women imparted to them a great deal of power within their families and communities. This power allowed women to make decisions and create and sell goods, since women were actively contributing to their families' income and survival, just as their male counterparts were. Without this trade, their families and the families of other women would not survive. Thus, individual families and the community as a whole relied heavily upon this trade. While the idea of private and public spheres was in play in the seventeenth and eighteenth centuries to signal where women and men belonged, this division did not close women off from the public realm entirely. As Ryan notes in her study of Oneida County, New York, during its frontier phase from approximately 1790 to 1820, it was acknowledged that women should not "assume a position of authority or prominence in the public chambers of church or government."[7] Despite this, however, the community did not expect that women were to be "sentenced to insulation in the family unit."[8] It was acknowledged that women played a role in the community and that they were active and contributing members. Additionally, Ryan points out that the meaning of "public" and "private" in this period is difficult to understand today.[9] She implies that the boundaries of these spheres appear to have been nebulous, allowing women and men to cross over into the sphere with which they were not associated and allowing, in the case mentioned above, women to play important roles in family survival and economic activity.

The theory that there was a permeable boundary between these two spheres is further developed by both Sara Evans, in her references to the same period, and by sociologist Karen Hansen, whose study of working class women and men in antebellum New England reveals a third sphere – or an area of blending of the public and private – in addition to the public and private spheres, called "the social."[10] The women played a role in the community not just through the trade of homemade goods, but also through women's constant visiting, gossiping, and coming together for community celebrations and religious services, in which the women played a role in their community's morality and even its politics. Through their interactions with one another and with men in the community, women were able to shape rules that governed everyone's daily lives, influence how people conducted themselves publicly and privately, and assist with the maintenance of the small primitive economy that existed within and between communities. Peer pressure, and what Ryan calls the "time-honored New England technique" of will-breaking, "suppressing the child's independent desires and self-assertions" that could start in infancy but continue with adults if they had not learned their lesson early on – were all examples of how women (and men) were able to shape their community and prevent too much individuality and autonomy, which could oppose the workings of a corporate community.[11] Everyone had to work together in order for the community and for families to survive, and women played a key role in this effort.

Colonial American "She-Merchants"

As the colonies expanded with greater numbers of people immigrating to America, and as the frontier was pushed farther inland, the need to live in a corporate family economy began to change. As populations grew, New England's small villages became large towns and then cities; their economies began to evolve. People were no longer living on a frontier; they were living in a small bustling town or city and the need for a family and a community to work together for their common survival no longer existed. What was once a "primitive economy" with a lack of cash and labor became something of the past.[12] By the late eighteenth century, new opportunities developed as industry and small factories began to expand, farming practices changed, and small businesses and shops opened to sell needed products. A greater divide opened between classes, as the wealthier merchants and their families no longer had to produce goods within the home and could purchase what they needed.[13] Some women found opportunities for work just as men did, particularly in the growing urban areas. Known as "she-merchants," these women ran small shops that catered to other women, such as millineries or clothiers.[14] Single and widowed women found sources of self-employment through dame schools, inns and taverns, or domestic service to support themselves and their families. Some widows even continued their husband's businesses, particularly if their husbands had been artisans. Before their spouses died, the women had helped to manage their husbands' businesses and likely worked side-by-side with their husbands, children, and assistants in the artisans' shop.[15] Thus, it was natural for them to continue the work.

Interestingly, despite the fairly extensive work of these widows and single women, a separation began to emerge between women's and men's spheres by the late eighteenth century. With more buying power and less home production needed, more men began to physically work outside the home. Colonies encouraged and even legislated that women should remain focused on the tasks within the home and the management of the household.[16] By the end of the eighteenth century, New England was no longer a frontier, but a prosperous region that was developing economically and industrially. However, there was at least one place in New England that retained the characteristics of the frontier for many reasons, but most notably because of its isolation.

Nantucket Island

The Founding of Nantucket Island

Seventeenth- and eighteenth-century Nantucket Island mirrored many of the trends of colonial American society, particularly with participation in a corporate family economy. The island was settled by whites in the fall of 1659. Inhabited by approximately 3,000 Wampanoag, Nantucket had been visited infrequently by whites. White visitation had occurred when inhabitants of Martha's Vineyard came to shear sheep that they left grazing year-round on the island or when they came to convert the native population to Christianity. One of these Vineyard residents sold the island to a group of men from the area of Salisbury, Massachusetts in 1659. They purchased the island in large part because of its isolation and the freedom this would afford them. The twenty "first purchasers," as they are often referred to, were seeking an alternative to the restrictions of Puritan society. Privacy was essential after leaving a place where neighbors were too close and seclusion non-existent; they craved privacy in order to live their lives freely. Several of the first purchasers had run into trouble in their communities. Among their indiscretions were different religious beliefs, refusal to pay taxes for the local church or minister, and in one instance, harboring Quakers.[17] Thus, the purchase was both a commercial investment and an escape from the religious and economic restrictions of the Puritan communities.

Like most settlers in early America, many pushed to find this frontier – a place they recognized as having freedom, whether it be religious, economic, political, or otherwise.

The Frontier Island: Autonomy and Freedom Found

Nantucket's first purchasers and the others who would follow over the next decades sought this frontier because of the promises it held. For the first purchasers of Nantucket, this frontier promised them a place of privacy, freedom, and independence, where the families could work together to succeed. By dividing up the living site along the harbor at Wesco into large lots with large expanses between each house, these settlers planned to live their lives in the way they wished, worship how they wished, and save their money. As scholar Edward Byers notes,

> Nantucket's English settlers seemed to share an activist
> mentality that encouraged a jealous sense of personal
> independence, impatience with restraint, and enlarged
> expectations for themselves and their children – an
> acquisitive temperament that today is labeled possessive
> individualism.[18]

Nantucket's settlers wanted to remove themselves from the restrictive communities that they had inhabited and to "continue the kind of economic activity that was part of their early colonial background"[19] – they were looking for a new frontier. Their lives would revolve around the corporate family economy – subsisting on what they produced off the land by farming – and also trading some of their crops to bring in other goods not produced on the island. Like the first Oneida County settlers studied by Ryan, the island settlers were living on a frontier where they had purchased their land – it was not inherited or granted in a colonial charter. By purchasing the land, Nantucket resembled Oneida County as "a patchwork of detached farms and dwelling units rather than a dense nucleated New England village."[20] The purchasers had the luxury of building their community in the way they saw fit and were not restricted to certain portions of land. The island acquired the appearance of a patchwork quilt with large tracts of land shaped in a hodgepodge fashion

14

and without a central square. This look underscores the fact that islanders did not meddle in one another's affairs and that the expanses between their homes and the lack of a tight, nucleated village served to illustrate their desire for privacy and their independent nature.

Unfortunately, the new islanders soon found that farming was not a viable option. The poor, sandy soil could not support the production of large expanses of crops, and the islanders were forced to find an alternative. With hundreds of acres of wild heath, sheep were the perfect match for the unruly moors. Sheep could be left to roam at will, feeding freely and safely without human oversight, because of the island's natural ocean boundaries and the absence of predators. With much of the land held in common, islanders did not have to worry about their sheep grazing on a neighbor's land and the attendant problems that this would have caused if they were living on the mainland. Thus sheep farming, coupled with growing food for basic sustenance, was the primary means of survival, although islanders still had to rely on trade with the mainland in order to attain some basic necessities. Despite this initially large reliance on the mainland, Nantucketers learned to live independently and to rely on their families and on one another. They reduced their reliance on the mainland and enforced the island's independence and autonomy by enticing others to make the island their home, offering them land in exchange for moving to the island and practicing their trade, such as blacksmithing, cod fishing, or shoe making.

An Island of "Benign Neglect"

Laws and regulations were few and far between – they had left mainland life in part because of strict laws – and people were free to practice whatever religion they chose. There were no established churches or religions on the island and Sundays were spent at a neighbor's home in a religious service led by an elder of that faith or spent roaming the moors on a "rantum scoot," a long walk or drive in a calash (cart).[21] With a considerable distance from their governing body – first New York and then Massachusetts – Nantucketers made their own decisions and acted independently. In fact, the islanders lived in what Byers calls a "state of benign neglect" by New York, not paying taxes or duties to the colonial government.[22] Visitation by governing officials was likely almost non-existent. On a good day with perfect wind, it likely took seven to eight hours just to reach some of the closer towns on Cape Cod. A trip to New York would have taken several days.

In his *Letters from an American Farmer* (1782), J. Hector St. John de Crèvecoeur, who visited the island in the late 1760s, noted the independent and autonomous nature of the island and her people. He stated,

> . . . their civil code is so light that it is never felt . . . .
> Nothing can be more simple than their municipal
> regulations, though similar to those of the other
> counties of the same province, because they are
> more detached from the rest, more distinct in their
> manners, as well as in the nature of the business
> they pursue, and more unconnected with the populous
> province to which they belong . . . . [23]

There was little to no oversight by a larger governmental power, thus further reinforcing the island's autonomy and the independence in which the islanders took great pride.

The "will-breaking" and refusal to allow for individuality to which Ryan refers in her study of Oneida County, New York, can be found to some extent on Nantucket, making up for the "light" civil code noted by Crèvecoeur. Until the first selectmen were elected in the early 1670s, there was no local government, and the leading males of the island community met together as issues arose that needed to be addressed concerning the island and its population of about three hundred whites and eight hundred Wampanoag.[24] They would seek out the troublemaker or address the issue at hand – it was a community effort. Once established, Nantucket had more local town meetings than any other town in New England at the time, still carefully guarding its local control and not allowing religious criteria to inform who voted – property ownership defined voting rights.[25] An "orderliness and decorum" were expected of islanders, although it was not enforced in the way the Puritan communities enforced behavior. Local courts created and enforced the laws – many of them involved in the areas of alcohol and regulating what they called "outsiders" – the Wampanoag and visitors to the island.[26]

While a diverse group of inhabitants, the community was close-knit and interdependent. Nantucketers needed to work together and be a united front, not only because of the isolation in which they lived, but also because of the possibility that the island's native population might revolt – which the Wampanoag never did, living for the most part in harmony with the white settlers, unlike some of their Wampanoag sisters and brothers on the mainland.[27] This important sense of independence and isolation reinforced the idea of the island as a frontier. This island frontier was better defined and more of a constant, unlike the arbitrary and temporary frontier of Oneida County, because the island would always remain isolated.

Quakerism

The Birth of the Religious Society of Friends

The freedoms and independence of island society and the way in which the islanders lived, with wives and husbands sharing in the support of the family and the community, allowed for the development and growth of a relatively new and unique religious sect. It was a Christian sect that believed it had "discovered . . . a new spiritual Principle . . . which . . . was destined to revolutionise (sic) life, society, civil government, and religion."[28] It was one that fit especially well with the independent nature of the island and her people, for the "English of the island were culturally Quaker . . . [they] were modest, hard-working, [and] respect[ed] women as leaders . . . ."[29]

Founded in England by George Fox in the 1650s, the Society of Friends, or Quakers as they would later be more commonly referred to, was a religious movement that was born in the era of Reformation Europe. From the start, the Society, like other Christian sects that developed in the period, met with opposition because "early Quakers challenged myriad theological and social conventions."[30] The sect's most challenging claim was its belief that God spoke directly to all people.

Quakers believed that God moved individuals from within to speak and
that all Christians should and could be ministers. Because of this belief,
the Friends did not utilize priests or official ministers in their meetings of
worship. No liturgy, ritual, or sacraments were given at a meeting.
Friends met in silent worship, "centering down" – pushing away worldly
cares, in many respects a form of meditation – to await what they
referred to as the "Inner Light." The Inner Light was the "seed" that was
found in every person, starting at birth. It was the presence of God.[31] If
they felt moved by this Inner Light, they would stand and share with the
rest of the meeting the words of God that were within them. Typically, it
was the elders or "ministers" of the meeting who did this. These people
were chosen by the meeting to act as leaders when necessary. Elders
were chosen for their piety and stability and "ministers" were chosen for
their ability to speak frequently with sufficient "attendance on the
Spirit."[32]

Because God spoke to everyone, Friends believed that everyone was
equal; there was no social hierarchy. Friends refused to use titles when
referring to people, instead using an individual's first name. They
opposed "displays and manifestations of social deference and respect,"[33]
choosing not to bow to people or doff their hats. Friends interpreted
portions of the Bible literally, refusing to take oaths or pledges, bear
arms, or make public displays of vanity, which resulted in their plain,
drab dress. They believed in the complete separation of church and state.

The one tenet of the faith that was most unnerving to religious and
governmental powers of the time was that the Friends believed that
women were the spiritual equals of men. Because of this belief, women
could minister to the people just as men did. Women became central to
the Quaker movement; many of the first converts to Quakerism were
women, and women made up a large percentage of ministers in the faith
who traveled to spread the word.[34] In the Quaker faith, women were
allowed to address public groups of people – both women and men –
something that was unacceptable because of its challenge to the
traditional place of women in mainland American society. Women's
role in society was heavily influenced throughout the colonies by the
Puritan interest in attaching "particular importance to regulating female

behavior."[35] The Quakers did not "regulate" their female members as they Puritans and other religious groups did.

The first Quaker to visit America was a female Friend. In 1655/56, Elizabeth Harris traveled to the Chesapeake Bay area, meeting with people who claimed to be Quakers and helping to establish these people and other converts in official Quaker meetings.[36] Over the next several years, more Quaker ministers came to the colonies to spread the word and were frequently confronted with violence, imprisonment, and in some cases, death. In particular, the Massachusetts Bay Colony was the most inhospitable and brutal colony for Quakers to visit or attempt to inhabit. Nevertheless, called by God to minister to the people, Friends continued to visit the colony, despite the violence and imprisonment they faced. Numerous Friends were disfigured or even hanged for attempting to convert people to Quakerism.[37] Often, those Friends who were banished from a town would return again and again, even knowing that they would certainly face death. But their calling by God was stronger. As a result of what the Puritans saw as a shocking behavior by Quakers, the Puritans believed that Quakers were possessed by the Devil.[38] Why else would Quakers return to a place from which they were banished, with the threat of whipping or death if they returned?

Women and the Quaker Faith

The Puritan society of Massachusetts felt threatened by the Friends, viewing Quaker beliefs as blasphemous and heretical. The Quaker religion was a direct challenge to the Puritan social order in that Quakers refused to defer to any authority, opposed taking oaths, and provided women with power and a public role.[39] Ironically, the first generation of Puritans had been more open to female involvement in the church and removed themselves to the American frontier in order to practice their religion freely and to allow women and men to live and worship "free from traditional restraints."[40] But when women tried to assert themselves and control religious doctrine, specifically where it related to themselves, the doors to the freedoms they initially found open were closed, and subsequent generations of Puritans became firm believers in the inferiority and submission of women.[41] They supported these beliefs with passages from the Bible: the sins committed by Eve when she disobeyed God and the words of Saint Paul that forbade women to speak in church and claimed that women were subordinate to men.[42] The belief in the subordination of women was further reinforced by church leaders and preached to the faithful by their ministers. This concept hearkens back to Ryan's discussion of the separation of public and private that allowed for some movement of women in the public sphere, but forbade their outspokenness or direct role in church or government. Within the Quaker faith, the lack of an authority further reinforced the ability of women to be perceived as equals to men.

Despite all the difficulties they faced, the Quakers persisted in their mission and in practicing their faith. In the late 1600s and again in the mid-1700s, they made changes to their doctrine in order to combat the persecution they faced and to garner more control of their membership – in particular the more exuberant members who traveled throughout the American colonies and drew negative attention to the religion. The belief that women and men were equals before God did not change, thus allowing women to speak in meeting and travel on behalf of their religious beliefs.

Interestingly, in many cases, the belief in female and male equality came from the same words that the Puritans used to deny it. Quakers believed that the "Inner Light" was a continuing revelation and "Friends could ignore ancient limitations on women by claiming that the new Light could, at a minimum, serve as a guide to understanding earlier revelations."[43] The same story of Eve used by the Puritans to illustrate female inferiority was utilized by Fox; he reinterpreted its meaning. According to Maples Dunn, Fox "considered the spiritual regeneration of the converted as a triumph over the curse," because men and women were equal before the fall and with rebirth, the equality returned.[44]

The Quaker Meeting of Worship

One of the first major steps to make Quakerism more acceptable to non-Quakers and to bring more uniformity to the religion was the establishment of formal meetings of worship. Meetings varied in their purpose and functions: there were local meetings for weekly worship; monthly business meetings; quarterly meetings whereby several meetings in a region would come together for business and worship; and yearly meetings where representatives from the quarterly meetings would gather for several days once per year. The establishment of the monthly business meeting would later allow for both a men's and a women's monthly business meeting (monthly meeting) where business was conducted at the conclusion of a shorter meeting of worship. By establishing a meeting for women, the Friends were further empowering the female members of the Society.

In their assemblies, women took care of the female members of the meeting. The women's monthly business meeting had special responsibilities, including reviewing of proposed marriages for the women, collecting money for the poor and Friends who had fallen upon difficult times, approving travel permits for women members, and helping to build the meetinghouses with the money they raised within their separate monthly business meeting. And in America, these monthly business meetings were physically separated, providing women with more privacy and control over the conduct of their meeting. As remembered by one Nantucket girl, Deborah Coffin Hussey Adams, "The men and women sat on opposite sides of the building with a low partition between them. Heavy shutters were let down when a business meeting was going on, completely separating the two parts of the house."[45]

Quakerism on Nantucket Island

"The Great Woman" and the Religious Society of Friends on Nantucket

On Nantucket, the early white community had no established religion. Individuals were free to worship how and when they wanted, and several different faiths were represented on the island. A series of visits by Quakers to Nantucket initiated the changes to the religious face of the island. As early as 1698, the first Quakers arrived on Nantucket after hearing that people on the island were inclined to the Quaker faith. The first Friend to visit was Thomas Chalkey, followed by John Richardson, and then Thomas Story.[46] Richardson was drawn to the household of one individual in particular – Mary Coffin Starbuck (1645–1719).

A leading fixture on the island, "Great Mary" or "the Great Woman" as she became known, held a unique position in the small island community.[47] Owner of the island trading post with her husband, Nathaniel Starbuck, Mary was in constant contact with her fellow islanders as they came to her to make purchases and pay down debt owed on previous purchases. With this power over the community, Mary was often sought for personal and business advice by her neighbors and customers and held a substantial amount of sway over them. Her legendary answer to many questions was, "My husband and I think . . ." but many knew that the statement made or opinion given was likely that of Mary Coffin Starbuck.[48] Her situation was additionally unique in that she was the only one of the husband and wife team who could read and write. Mary controlled the account books and all paperwork associated with the family business. She was a she-merchant and "a woman of strong magnetic personality and extraordinary administrative ability . . . [who] . . . possessed a genius for participating in public, social, and domestic duties.[49]

When Richardson arrived on the island, he knew that Mary already had tendencies toward the Quaker faith and that she had inspired others on the island to join her in informal meetings at her home.[50] Both Richardson and Story saw a leader in Mary and felt she was the only one on the island who could shape and lead a meeting, assuring its survival.[51] These "radical spiritists," as they were referred to, while not necessarily an organized religion, had similar beliefs to the Quakers. And, like Quakers, their "wide variety of religious, social, and political ideas . . . alarmed most seventeenth-century New Englanders"[52] – but not on Nantucket, where religious freedom and tolerance was the norm. It was with Mary's assistance, and the use of her home, that Richardson and other Quaker ministers would influence the conversion of many Nantucketers to Quakerism. Because of her power within the community and her own family, the Quaker faith seemed a logical match for this powerful woman because it allowed her to maintain her position of authority and independence and also reinforced it. According to scholar Lisa Norling, "Mary Starbuck's convincement suggests the appeal of Quaker belief to powerful women."[53] Since the island did not welcome Puritanism, the religion that they had been trying to escape, Mary and other island women were able to establish themselves with high status and independence that they found in this frontier place.

Establishment of Quaker Meeting on Nantucket

Established as a weekly meeting with seventy-five adults and thirty children by 1704, the Friends meeting was the only organized religious body on the island,[54] which then had a white population that numbered approximately three hundred.[55] In 1708, Nantucket meeting applied for the establishment of a monthly meeting for the women and men. Nine persons signed the petition which was recorded on the first page in "A Record of the Births, Deaths, Receptions, Disownments & Removals, Alphabetically Arranged in the Society of Friends on the Island of Nantucket" – a book kept by the first official meeting of Friends on the island beginning in 1708. Those who signed the petition included Mary Coffin Starbuck and Nathaniel, Anna Trott, Jethro Starbuck, Dorcas Starbuck, and Priscilla Coleman.[56] Of the four women who signed, Anna is not shown as having a husband who signed the petition. One can deduce that she was single, widowed, or unmarried, but in any case, she was a woman signing alone within Quaker meeting, illustrating the equality of women within the meeting. Four of the petitioners were Quaker ministers, two of them women – Mary Coffin Starbuck and Priscilla Coleman.[57] Yearly Meeting in Rhode Island recognized and approved the establishment of a Nantucket Monthly Meeting exclusively for men.[58] This was not because Yearly Meeting opposed having a women's meeting. Still relatively new in its establishment, Rhode Island Yearly was all male and could not grant the establishment of a women's monthly meeting because it had no women who could do this.

"Great Mary" and her fellow female Friends did not let this stop them. As the men met in their first monthly meeting, Mary – likely the instigator – and the other women, met at Parliament House (Mary's home) for their own religious meeting. In a book bound in sheepskin, in a feminine hand, is the following statement from that meeting:

> Our yearly meeting of women friends Held 28th
> 4 mo 1708 on nantucket – At the house of Nathaniel
> Starbuck And wee had a good meeting feeling
> the power of the lord [unknown word] [unknown
> word] Amongst us it is Concluded by this meeting
> that there shall be a monthly meeting kept the last
> second day of Every month in the yeare.[59]

The women were moved by God to form their own meeting, without consent of their male counterparts, without consent by Yearly Meeting. And since it was God's will, in 1708 the Women's Nantucket Monthly meeting was established and accepted by both the men's meeting on Nantucket and the Yearly Meeting in Rhode Island.

The first book in the Women's Monthly Meeting has a sheepskin cover with "The Monthly Meeting Book of Women Friends" lightly written across the cover. It could be in the hand of Mary Coffin Starbuck, and could even be an account book that she sold in her store. For the first decade or so, the minutes kept by the Women's Monthly Meeting were short, noting the dates of the meeting, money collected most likely for the poor but possibly also for the future building of a meetinghouse, and several single line mentions of marriage intentions by members of meeting and the appointment of individuals to check for the "clearness" of an intended wife and husband. The act of the women's establishment of their own meeting flew in the face of the normal practices of seventeenth and early eighteenth century American society. Women in colonial America could participate to some extent in the public part of life in the seventeenth and eighteenth centuries, but were not allowed to act within the realm of religion as they were doing on Nantucket as Quakers. Nantucket women were given substantial responsibilities and power within their religion. They acted independently from men.

world at bay and living in a state of isolation.

The Quaker Influence on Nantucket Island

The Quaker faith continued to grow and influence even the non-Quakers who inhabited the island. In 1728, the population of whites on the island numbered approximately 917 persons; the number of Quakers was 359.[71] Between 1700 and 1750, the population of the island grew from three hundred whites to approximately three thousand.[72] An increasing number of Quakers served in local government and Quaker leaders within meeting became leaders within the town. Quakers became some of the elite in political life on the island, bringing them social status among their peers.[73] Between 1760 and 1769, 71.4 percent of the men who served as town selectmen were Quakers, compared with no Congregationalists and 28.6 percent marked as men of unknown religious affiliation who served as selectmen in that period.[74] To place this into better perspective, the known number of Quakers on the island in 1758 was 1,173 and the number of island whites was 3,320 in 1764. By the time a new Quaker meetinghouse was erected in 1764, the building had the capacity to seat two thousand members.[75] Certainly this rise within politics and society illustrated that the Quakers were indeed living "in the light." God was rewarding them for their hard work by making them prosperous within their community, not just with money but also with an important role to play in the shaping of their community.

With this growing influence in the local community, the Quaker religion could be found pervading the laws and society of the island community – it was willingly accepted by the non-Quakers even as far as how many of them dressed and how all dwellings were built on the island – plainly and simply. As Crèvecoeur noted concerning the homes of islanders: "they are all of a similar construction and appearance, plain and entirely devoid of exterior or interior ornament."[76] The author further noted the growing influence of the Quakers on the small island society when he stated, "The manners of the Friends are entirely founded on that simplicity which is their boast and their most distinguishing characteristic, and those manners have acquired the authority of laws"[77] on the island.

Both in their architecture and dress, all Nantucketers illustrated the Quaker ethic of simplicity. If one acted in an ostentatious manner, that person was frowned upon for being frivolous. Similarly to Ryan's discussion of will-breaking which was found in the frontier's family-based economy, the Quakers and Nantucketers found ways to make people conform. "Through the use of social ostracism and ridicule, the community informally enforced its system of values" on Quakers and non-Quakers alike.[78] Simplicity fit well with a place where, despite their ability for self-reliance, the latest fashions and even wood to build their homes must come from the mainland and were thus expensive.

Sarah Barney: A Quaker Woman's Influence in the World's Quaker Community

The belief that women were equals to men within the Quaker meeting migrated to more general island society. The ability of Quaker women to manage their own finances within meeting, their ability to make rules associated with their female members, and the allowance of their female members to travel and to speak out in meetings deeply influenced non-Quaker women and men on the island. The same record book that holds the record of the first women's meeting on Nantucket reveals further the ways in which women were treated equally to men within Quaker meeting. The book holds the travel requests and copies of the letters of certification – similar to a passport – of members who were going on extended breaks from the island and who wished to attend meeting elsewhere. Additionally, there are requests and certifications for those who felt called by God to leave the island to minister in different communities, to share the word of God with other Quakers, and to assist in converting non-Quakers.

A well-known, unmarried Quaker woman on Nantucket, Sarah Barney made such a request on the twenty-second day of the second month 1762 to the Women's Monthly Meeting to travel abroad in England. On the twenty-ninth day of the third month 1762, the meeting approved her request and copied the letter certifying her clearness for the trip into the meeting's records. It is addressed, "To Friends in Great Britain or where these may come" and states:

> *Dear Friends Our Esteemed friend Sarah*
> *Barney Having laid before this Meeting a*
> *Concern resting upon her mind to accompany*
> *our worthy Friend Comfort Hoag in a Religious*
> *visit to your parts; and requesting of us a few lines*
> *by way of Certificate. These are to certify on her*
> *Behalf that she is a Friend in good unity with us*
> *and that she is of a sober life & conversation . . .*
> *we do hereby Recommend her unto you . . . .[79]*

Barney would travel for more than fifty years in the name of seeking rights for women Friends. Sarah Barney traveled in part to press for the development of more women's meetings, particularly in England, where British Quakers lagged behind the American Friends. In 1761, fifty-three years after Mary Coffin Starbuck and other women friends were denied a women's monthly meeting because Rhode Island Yearly did not have one,[80] Barney helped to establish the New England Yearly Meeting of Women Friends after seeking the assistance of Philadelphia Yearly Meeting that, like Nantucket, had a Women's Yearly Meeting. Barney would also use this Philadelphia support to press London to create a women's meeting.[81] Obviously, Barney was a noted member of Quaker meeting and her work and travels could not have gone unnoticed in the small island community. Her status as a single woman freed her from the need to attend to a family, but many married Quaker women who traveled left infants and children behind in the care of family members or friends while they traveled to minister. One wonders what sort of an example Barney might have set for other island women, particularly non-Quakers, and the young girls in the community. Sarah Barney was not the only woman of late eighteenth-century Nantucket who stands out as an example of how Nantucket women enjoyed freedoms and equality to men. This independence would grow as the whalefishery developed on the island and the Quaker faith continued to flourish.

Independent and Autonomous Nantucket and Its Pioneer Women

Economic Changes on Nantucket

Throughout the eighteenth century, Nantucket continued to evolve as a community and as an economy. The whalefishery was developing. Based first upon what they were taught by the Wampanoag concerning driftwhaling in the late 1600s, Nantucketers realized that whaling could be their economic mainstay if they could more efficiently hunt and process the oil of the massive mammal. Their sense of community and common purpose was further developed with whaling. While the rest of the American colonies began to suffer in the mid- to late-eighteenth century, particularly because of Britain's stranglehold on them, Nantucket's Quaker work ethic and the new occupation of whaling allowed the island's economy to grow and prosper in this period.[82] As eighteenth-century author Hector St. John de Crèvecoeur noted, it was the island's "5,000 hardy people who boldly derive[d] their riches from the element that surround[ed] them and have been compelled by the sterility of the soil to seek abroad for the means of subsistence."[83] (The population was closer to 4,200 by the date Crèvecoeur was on the island.)[84] With the men turning to the sea and the women remaining behind onshore, women began to take on even greater tasks on the island than they ever had before.

Kezia Coffin: Infamous Loyalist She-Merchant and Independent Nantucket Woman in the Era of the American Revolution

Families played an important role not just within the Quaker faith but also within any society that relied on all members to work together for survival. On Nantucket, women played a dominant role in the family, especially because of the children and the need to educate them to be good moral people. In addition to this necessity, the Quakers needed to mold their children to the Quaker religion and way of life.[85]

> In order to provide for and maintain their
> families during the absence of their husbands,
> many eighteenth-century Nantucket women

30

went beyond traditional female activities to
manage family and business finances and engage
independently in some line of trade.[86]

It was Quakerism, the independent nature of islanders, and life on a
frontier with everyone working toward a common goal that allowed
Nantucket women to take a step further in the work that they did.

*One Quaker woman who serves as an example of engaging
independently in trade – perhaps in the extreme – was Kezia Folger
Coffin (1723 – 1798), a cousin of Benjamin Franklin. Nantucket's
infamous she-merchant, or she-pirate as she was sometimes referred to,
was a strong-willed woman. Crèvecoeur, who presumably met Kezia
and her husband, believed that*

> *the richest person now in the island owes
> all his present prosperity and success to the
> ingenuity of his wife . . . she laid the foundation
> of a system of business that she has ever since
> prosecuted with equal dexterity and success . . . .[87]*

*Kezia began to develop her business ventures while her husband was at
sea. He would later return to the island and give up the seaman's life,
but Kezia continued her pursuits, supporting their family. Kezia
developed and ran numerous successful enterprises, including opening
shops, conducting trade, purchasing ships for her own trade, and buying
shares in merchant ships. Additionally, she was the only Nantucket
agent who represented a leading London trading house.[88]*

The Nantucket economy boomed while the economy of the rest of the
colonies suffered as the American Revolution crept closer. Nantucket
continued to find ways to survive, even finding a way to exempt itself
from strict laws in Massachusetts that were imposed by Britain and
caused much economic strife for Massachusetts colonists. Nantucket
struck deals with both the British and the American governments in order
to continue trading, fishing, and some whaling in support of its
population now numbering 4,412 white persons by the eve of the
Revolution.[89]

Unfortunately, Nantucket suffered because of these agreements – the rest of the colonies saw the islanders as Loyalists and treated them as traitors because of their independent dealings with the British. Nantucketers simply did what they always had done – they made their own rules and independent decisions, and they attempted to remain neutral in the conflict. This stemmed not just from their independent attitude or their remote location, but also from the Quaker belief in pacifism that pervaded their society.

They relied upon the sea for their livelihood and trade, and since Britain controlled the sea – Nantucket had to act accordingly to survive – another mentality of living on a frontier. Scholar Edward Byers notes that the

> community's 'islandness' contributed to its non-
> involvement. Nantucketers conceived of the island
> community as a place apart, with its own values
> and traditions; a conception that insulated it as
> surely as did the sea. Despite their cosmopolitanism,
> Nantucketers conceived of their duties and based
> their actions on parochial and familial concerns. They
> neither anticipated nor wanted the break with Britain
> and resented the outside influences that the Revolution
> brought to bear. Such attitudes were certainly not
> confined to Nantucket, but its history and 'detached'
> condition intensified them. The 'nation of Nantucket'
> had always remained aloof and distanced from provincial
> affairs, except to pay for and make use of provincial authority
> when it suited the island's needs.[90]

While not a Loyalist island, there were British sympathizers and Kezia was herself a Loyalist. Although islanders suffered because of the conditions they had created due to their "possessive individualism," Kezia with her quick business mind and her connections to the British, and some say, smugglers, was able to make a fortune. Kezia rode along with the thriving island economy before the war, becoming one of the most successful merchants on the island.

During the war, Kezia held a monopoly over trade on Nantucket. Nantucketers who were facing hard times due to the war found themselves resigned to borrowing money or receiving credit from Kezia. This left her with liens on the homes and businesses of her fellow islanders, as well as on the wharves and warehouses of other island merchants.[91] As her monopoly and her wealth grew, so did an uproar among her fellow islanders regarding her business practices. Kezia and her close male cohorts saw nothing wrong with working with the British in order to secure goods for the island. Kezia, in particular, would take advantage of her fellow islanders by charging high prices for goods that only she could provide due to her connections.

While an infamous figure, Kezia is a perfect illustration of the strength of character and the independent nature of Nantucket women. Unfortunately, few primary sources exist from the eighteenth century concerning Kezia or her sister Nantucketers. A few documents exist that are dated from after the American Revolution and they help to further tell the story of Kezia and her power. She and several other men, her previously mentioned cohorts, were put on trial for treason. They were prosecuted because it was believed that they were "persons dangerous, and criminal to the freedom and independence of this and the other United States of America; as Encouragers, Aiders and Abettors of Enemy."[92] Further, it was found that the accused had made attempts "to induce the inhabitants of said Island, to settle correspondence with and openly join the Enemy."[93] If they were found guilty, death was the punishment. Kezia was the only woman in the group, and even more telling, her husband, John Coffin, was not named as a part of the incident. The charges were finally dropped. When Nantucket eventually claimed neutrality in the Revolution, in great part to ease the difficulties the island was having with trade and travel, Kezia lost her monopoly because other merchants were able to trade more freely and without threat of injury to their crews, ships, or goods.

In the end, Kezia went bankrupt and was forced to sell off her numerous homes, warehouses, and the rest of her holdings. Legend has it that her neighbors took turns attending the auctions so that only one person was there to bid; thus, Kezia's holdings sold at rock bottom prices. When her home was repossessed, Kezia was supposedly carried out on her chair because she refused to leave. After she and the others were charged and tried at Watertown, Massachusetts for smuggling and aiding the British, Kezia returned to the island with one purpose: to sue the Town and its people for taking away all of her possessions. Her lawyer son-in-law told her that her plan would never succeed, but Kezia supposedly said that she did not necessarily want to win. The legend is that her intent was to tie everything up in court and allow it to drag on for as long as possible. One scholar believes she may have been the inventor of the harassing lawsuit.[94]

A controversial figure, Kezia Coffin was a woman who functioned independently from her husband and provided for her family. She did this in an environment where women worked outside and within the home and where society condoned this activity. While she was later disowned by Quaker meeting, in part because of her purchase of a spinet (a small piano-like instrument) for her daughter, Kezia was like Mary Coffin Starbuck – an island woman of force. Little remains of her own words. Historians rely on the partial diary of her daughter Kezia Coffin Fanning – often referred to as Kezia Junior – and other small pieces of information, including a nineteenth-century novel Miriam Coffin, or the whale-fishermen, (only subtly fictionalized) that revolves around Kezia and her misdeeds, and the words of Crèvecoeur.

Kezia was a woman acting with complete independence and functioning in a dominant role in her community in a time when women elsewhere in the American colonies – particularly those of the middling and upper classes – were slowly finding that the door that once allowed them some movement between the private and public spheres was closing on them and beginning to relegate them to the home more and more. While she angered her island community because of her selfishness and the fact that she took advantage of them, they were not angered because she was a woman doing this. They were angered because she took advantage of them, and many suffered because of her actions. Despite the fact that she was devious and unfair, Kezia was acting in an independent and autonomous way – just as she was taught by living on her island nation. She might have left out the rest of the community, allowing them to

34

suffer, and not acting with a mind toward a corporate family economy, but her actions were fostered by the frontier mentality of the island and were given the opportunity to grow unfettered.

A Revolution: For Quaker and Non-Quaker Women

Kezia was a powerful and wealthy she-merchant who played a significant role in Nantucket's wartime economy. Mainland women during the American Revolution played significant roles within their communities, although possibly not to the extent that Kezia did. According to scholar Sara Evans, women participated in boycotts and even took on the work of their husbands if they were off fighting. There is evidence that some women were camp followers – often wives – who followed their husbands' companies providing meals, laundry services, and in some cases serving as nurses for the wounded. While excluded from politics, women still exhibited "the same revolutionary zeal," even though the Revolution "reinforced the view that political activities and aims were male."[95] Women of all walks of life found ways to contribute and influence what was happening. While many Quakers in urban areas showed British sympathies before the war (as appears to some degree with Nantucket, although that was mainly for survival), a tightening of the Quaker discipline in the 1750s forced Quakers in urban areas, such as Philadelphia and Providence – which was home to the New England Yearly Meeting – to follow the pacifist tenet of the faith. The Quakers in urban areas came to exhibit the Quaker tendencies of the Friends living in rural areas – that of pacifism and maintaining the membership levels of the meeting by better educating members concerning the faith. These changes in the Quaker faith, specifically the tightening of the Discipline, would later cause problems within the religion, but for the eighteenth century it bolstered the community connections of the Quakers.

While other colonial Quakers struggled with their pacifist beliefs, because of where they lived and what confronted them in the war, particularly their safety and the safety of their neighbors and way of life, Nantucketers remained relatively safe in their isolation. Their one struggle was that despite neutrality, Nantucketers found that their ships were being seized by *both* the Americans and the British, causing difficulties for getting goods to and from the islands.

The island's reliance on whaling dissipated because of the difficulties during the American Revolution, but soon after the war was over Nantucketers returned to the sea in search of the mammal that brought them world-wide fame and status as the whaling capital of the world. They were able to rebuild the fleet that had suffered due to the numerous consequences of war. The search for their massive prey would take Nantucket men farther out to sea and keep them away for longer periods of time. As a result, women found more opportunities to continue to work outside the home, further developing their own enterprises, and taking the place of their husbands while they were away at sea. This unique situation grew over the course of the eighteenth century and became even more prominent in the nineteenth century. As Crèvecoeur noted in his *Letters from an American Farmer,*

> As the sea excursions are often very long, their wives in their absence are necessarily obliged to transact business, to settle accounts, and, in short, to rule and provide for their families. These circumstances, being often repeated, give women the ability as well as a taste for that kind of superintendency, to which, by their prudence and good management, they seem to be in general very equal. This employment ripens their judgment and justly entitles them to a rank superior to that of other wives . . . . The men at their return . . . cheerfully give their consent to every transaction that has happened during their absence . . . 'Wife, thee hast done well,' is the general approbation . . . .[96]

The idea of women ruling the island and their families was noted in many histories, fiction, and poetry. In the late nineteenth century, native islander and groundbreaking female astronomer Maria Mitchell wrote a poem about one of her students who was from Nantucket with several lines making note of the power of island women stating, "She was born where women rule."[97]

Judith Macy: Island Entrepreneur

With the growth of whaling, the island saw the increased development of women taking charge of family businesses, managing family finances, and becoming entrepreneurs, whether they opened shops downtown, ran shops out of their homes, or produced goods in their own homes to sell and sometimes trade to others. While this female management and entrepreneurship developed strongly in the nineteenth century, it was rooted in what began in the eighteenth century. Women were keeping the island economy afloat. Kezia Coffin's sister, Judith Macy (1729 – 1819), was one such eighteenth-century entrepreneur. Unlike many of her sister islanders however, Judith's husband was at home.

Widowed after just two years of marriage, Judith then married second husband, Caleb Macy, a man who had faced many financial failures in his short life. Like most island men, Caleb had gone to sea but "'found his health incompetent to the hardships of a seafaring life.'"[98] According to their son Obed, Caleb found not just a life partner and someone to tend to their household and children in his marriage to Judith, but he also found someone to help him in his business dealings. With ten children and her husband's shoemaking business to assist in, Judith found herself taking care of several men who boarded with the family. Sometimes as many as twelve men joined her family of ten children at the dinner table. These men were likely Caleb's workers. In her daybook, which is in the collection of the Nantucket Historical Association, Judith kept a fairly detailed, if sometimes scattered, account of items purchased and sold, work completed, and records concerning her boarders between 1784 and 1805. Judith employed at least one of her daughters and several other women to spin wool, which she sold for profit. In some cases, it appears that Judith hired out a daughter to do work, and she sold goods to her sons, several of whom were prosperous island merchants, including Obed.

The details of the lives of Judith and her sister, Kezia Coffin, and Mary Coffin Starbuck serve as some of the few examples of what life was like for women and the role they played in society and the island economy on Nantucket in the eighteenth century. In reference to her boarders,

Judith kept details of when they "came here to bord (sic)" and the number of meals they ate during the week. For example, on the fifteenth day of the sixth month 1800, Judith recorded that boarder Daniel Gifford "Eat 2 meals this week" and on the sixth day of the seventh month 1800, he "Eate (sic) 7 meals this week." Judith "sold corn out of the crib," nails, molasses, "scanes of yarn" – likely created in her home by herself, her daughters, and other women she hired – and candles.[99] She even made a record of candles that she sold to her son Silvanus. Judith seems to have played the role of supplier and seller for Silvanus, selling wool for him and making him sign off on his acceptance of the payment by having him make a notation in her daybook.

Judith's daybook served not just as a record of what was happening, but also as an account book for what she and people in her employ produced, what she sold, and her other income-producing activities. She kept track in her daybook of how many hours people worked for her and on her behalf for others. It also appears that she may have made loans to people so that they could pay the rent on their homes. Judith Macy even kept a detailed tally of personal items she loaned to others – surprisingly, even noting the items she loaned to her own children. Judith's husband obviously did not disapprove of her work since she continued working for so many years – almost right until her death, it appears. Meager evidence indicates that Caleb's shoemaking business was successful, and he owned a large amount of real estate on the island, so he did not need his wife to work.

Unlike her sister, Judith was a Quaker in good stead – serving on various committees, even serving as the clerk of the Women's Meeting. Thus, her Quaker beliefs and those of her husband may have furthered her ability to conduct so much business as a woman. Judith may have been influenced in part by her sister's entrepreneurial skills, but she was also living in a community that did not believe in idleness and needed everyone to work so that the island, its people, and its economy could survive. In some respects, the island took this frontier style of life even further, allowing women to take on important roles within the community.

With men at sea, pragmatism was needed – women had to manage the island's economic affairs or else the economy and the island nation would crumble with no one to fill the role while the men were at sea. This island continued to rely on the tightly knit corporate family economy – a family that incorporated most islanders as they were almost all related – and to support the practice of women working and leading within the community. The allowance for women to move freely within the public sphere of society was something that had only been partially available to women in the colonial frontier. On Nantucket, where it was coupled with isolation, a predominant Quaker religion, and a fierce independence as a community, it allowed island women to play important and powerful roles within the community, not just within their families.

Nantucket-born Lucretia Coffin Mott (1793 – 1880), whose mother owned a dry goods shop on the island in the late eighteenth century before the family moved off island, was just one of many islanders who noted this phenomenon when she said,

> . . . my mother . . . was actively engaged in
> the mercantile business, often going to
> Boston . . . . The exercise of women's talents
> in this line, as well as the general care which
> developed upon them, in the absence of their
> husbands, tended to develop and strengthen them
> mentally and physically.[100]

Nantucket women were abandoned and sometimes widowed by the call of whaling. They rose to the occasion not only by supporting themselves and their families, but also by taking over family businesses, opening their own businesses, and maintaining the island's booming economy. They had to do this to survive, but they also could do this because of the frontier life that existed on the island and because of the equality-based religion that pervaded the small community.

Nantucket's Seventeenth and Eighteenth Century Women: Mothers of Nantucket's and America's Future Women Leaders

Nantucket was a frontier in the seventeenth and eighteenth

centuries – a place where families and the community worked together for common survival and where island women found a place to exercise their entrepreneurial skills and lead because of the Quaker religion, the geographical isolation, and the frontier reliance on a corporate family economy. While some of the women's abilities developed because men were at sea, the "detached society"[101] allowed the island to exist as a frontier where women and men worked together for a common goal: survival. While the rest of New England lost its frontier status and women became more relegated to the domestic or private sphere, Nantucket women throughout the eighteenth century were just beginning to realize their potential as leaders. In the nineteenth century, Nantucket women and their place within island society attracted greater notice from outsiders. Those women not only further developed their capacity to lead, conduct business, and manage finances, they also reached out from the shores of Nantucket to influence other women, serving as women leaders in the sciences, educational and reform movements, and religions across the country. By the early twentieth century, they would be heralded and it would be noted that, "No other community in America of the size of Nantucket has ever given to the country so many extraordinary women."[102]

These "daring daughters," the children of a tiny isolated community, acknowledged and accepted the sometimes difficult situation in which they lived, using it to their own advantages and in the assistance of their families, neighbors, and their island home. What they learned from the life they led and from the other women around them gave them the courage and strength to move out into the larger world where, in many cases, women were restricted and limited as far as what they could do outside the home and the influence they could wield within their communities and their churches. As is further illustrated in Part Two, Nantucket women of the eighteenth and nineteenth centuries helped to set the pace for a continuing independence and freedom for their daughters, granddaughters, and great-granddaughters. Their actions were supported into the next century as the Quaker religion continued to influence the island, whaling continued to drive the economy, and Nantucket continued to be an isolated patch of sand off the coast of Cape Cod.

Part Two – "A Practical, Forceful Type of Woman:" Nantucket Women in the Age of Woman's Sphere

I have made up my mind now to be a Sailor's wife,

To have a purse full of money and a very easy life,

For a clever sailor husband is so seldom at his home,

That his wife can spend the dollars with a will that's all her own,

Then I'll haste to wed a sailor, and send him off to sea,

For a life of independence is the pleasant life for me . . . .

But when he says Goodbye my love, I'm off across the sea,

First I'll cry for his departure, then laugh because I'm free . . . .

From *The Nantucket Girl's Song*, 1855
(NHA Coll. 220, Log 136)

When this poem was penned in February 1855 near Russell, New Zealand in a company of four women – three of whom were the wives of Nantucket whaling captains – they were likely lonesome for the family and friends they left at home in order to make a long and dangerous voyage to be by the sides of their husbands. At the same time, they were possibly overwhelmed with joy to see their fellow Nantucket sisters. While it is not known with certainty who penned the poem, the writer reveals the idea that Nantucket women were living a life that was different from their American counterparts. Perhaps after being on the whaleship – a man's world – for so long a time, the three Nantucket wives longed for the life they had left behind.

While possibly lonely, sad, and stressed with their husbands away at sea for three to five years, life for women left behind on Nantucket was largely one of freedom and independence, both socially and economically. They were not all cloistered within the home tending hearthside and children, as many women in America were expected to be during the nineteenth century. Their small families, the continuing religious influence of the Quaker faith, the isolation of the island and its frontier status, combined with the fact that many men were away at sea for these long periods, provided Nantucket women with unique opportunities throughout the eighteenth and nineteenth centuries. It set them apart from women elsewhere in America because they took over family finances and businesses, held a variety of both professional and non-professional jobs, and started their own businesses, thus keeping the island's economy afloat and providing for their families.

Nantucket women accomplished this in a period when other maritime communities were witnessing the closing of doors that had once been open to women in the eighteenth century. Nantucket women were working in "a man's world," when the belief among the leaders of American society was that women should not work but should instead take care of their families and the home. This idea of a separate sphere permeated American society. Although it was the ideal, there were cases of women working – the growing manufactories are a case in point – but these women typically were of the lower classes, and those higher up in society looked down upon them because of their need to work. Working women did exist and in many cases were respected among their peers but again, their situation was not the ideal of American society. It was on Nantucket, a frontier-minded community even in the nineteenth century, that women made a unique mark, not only on their island home, but also on American society as well.

The Nineteenth Century and Woman's Sphere

The Theory of "Woman's Sphere"

By the late eighteenth and early nineteenth centuries, the social and economic climate was changing in America. With the development of industry, the growth of factories, and more efficient methods of farming, the economy was rapidly growing and expanding. The act of a family working together as a unit for survival and its close interaction with the rest of the community on a frontier began to come to an end as places developed economically and populations grew – ending a community's frontier status. More and more in developed areas, the family was becoming a self-contained unit in which the husband left the home to earn money and the wife remained behind to raise the children and tend to the household. Women were becoming more confined and less of an essential component to the family's survival. Home production continued for many, particularly in the lower classes, and women in higher classes managed their households. But with products that were once homemade, homegrown, or traded with a neighbor available in the local marketplace, both women and men were becoming freed from the corporate family economy that had been so prevalent in the pre-Revolutionary War era. This would open the door for some women to work in professional and non-professional occupations, but their numbers were limited and, in some cases, did not reflect as large a percentage of a local population as was represented on Nantucket.

Men were seeking opportunities outside the family and home. In need of cash to purchase the goods being manufactured, men had to head out to earn their buying power. Women's work that was once so integral to the family's survival was downgraded and not as highly valued. Items they once made at home like candles, soap, and spun yarn and other needs could be purchased in the marketplace. Some women from many levels of society still continued to make these and other goods at home, but the point was that they could now more easily purchase these goods. Children were no longer helping to the extent that they once did within and around the home. Their work was not as necessary for the family to survive.

Children – particularly boys – were the future of the growing nation and because of this needed proper upbringing. Women needed to see to the good, moral upbringing of the nation's future generations. Remaining at home focused on the children and hearth kept them from participating in a family economy, and with this, the corporate family economy and even the frontier began to fade. This is not to say that a frontier was lost in America. It did still exist – it was sweeping across the nation as the country expanded and new territories were settled far from the new cities of the East. By the late nineteenth century, much of the frontier would be gone due to expansion and improved transportation. With improved transportation and new technologies, better access to markets developed and goods from all over could be acquired by anyone from anywhere. It was these changes that brought about what scholars have often referred to as "woman's sphere" – a place where women were separated from the chaotic, immoral, and power-driven world of men.[103]

The idea of this theory of woman's sphere was first described by scholar Barbara Welter in 1966, with her ideas concerning the "cult of true womanhood." Welter was the first historian to illustrate that by the early nineteenth century upper class women were hostages in their own homes. Welter found that the popular and widespread practice in American society by this time was for women to remain at hearthside, tending to the home and children, and providing a refuge from the outside world that was developing quickly into a negative and immoral place. Welter utilized popular writings, sermons, religious tracts, and other literature of the period – much of it written by men – to illustrate that women and men were beginning to live in separate worlds. Over the last forty years, Welter's theory concerning this separate world has been expanded upon, and historians have turned to the letters, journals, and other documents written by women of the period to better illustrate how and why a separate sphere developed. This separate sphere grew largely in reaction to the changes in society that came with the development of a market-based economy and the loss of the corporate family economy.

With the changes in society and the need for women to educate the young males of the family to be good, moral citizens who would combat the evils that society was now creating, women needed to be able to teach their children, to provide moral inspiration, and to serve as examples for their husbands. As a result, women were allowed to pursue better educations, but they still found themselves cloistered away at female academies, seminaries, and women's colleges. They were isolated from the communities in which their schools were located and lived a regimented life that kept them in an environment similar to the one they had left at home. Even their relationships with their female instructors and professors were modeled on a mother-daughter relationship. While students began to rebel, asserting their independence and right to make their own decisions, this was still done from within the walls of their schools – a world that was a separate environment, a sphere or bubble, that was female-focused and kept the male world at bay.

Even young women from more rural areas who could not go to school and who were hired by the growing manufactories found themselves constricted by a life of strict rules and isolation. They were housed in boarding houses run by or condoned by the company for which they worked – male workers did not face this same sort of regulation. While their earnings and distance from home allowed them some autonomy and buying power, they too were still cloistered to some extent. Their low pay and the restrictions on how they lived kept them subordinate as society dictated, according to scholar Alice Kessler-Harris. They may have become highly socialized, independent, and successful at organizing some of the first "turn-outs" (strikes) in factories as scholar Thomas Dublin notes, but often they returned to their hometowns and families where they married and settled down, leaving behind the mills and the bit of independence they had in these bustling mill towns and cities like Lowell, Massachusetts. The idea that a woman could remain unmarried and without a home and children was not endorsed or revered by this "new" culture.

Going Backwards: The Loss of Opportunities for Women after the American Revolution

By 1840, scholar Gilda Learner believes, all of American society had changed. Women were no longer active in the democracy as they were in the colonial period and in the era of the American Revolution, when more opportunities were available for women. Once independence was won, women and their work were less necessary. With the growing changes in industry and the economy, women's work outside the home was no longer acceptable, and their role as active participants in the economy was small to non-existent. Learner states "their actual situation had in many respects deteriorated"[104] – they had gone backwards. Women had lost the independence and equality they had gained since coming to the New World. The women who worked fulltime for a wage after this point were mainly those who had to because they were poor and their work was needed for the family's survival. And, much of their work required little or no skill. The key was that women, in particular those in New England and along the more developed East Coast, were no longer living on a frontier – poor women had been left behind economically and what they were doing was no longer socially acceptable in non-frontier places. The ideal was to have enough money so that a middle or upper class woman could stay home to tend hearth and children and right the wrongs of the now immoral world from within their cloistered and safe environment.

As the frontier way of life left the east and moved westward, even the roles of midwives and nurses diminished as more doctors appeared in the rapidly growing towns and medicine became professionalized. Women were gradually replaced by professional doctors who now claimed the birth of children and minor illnesses as areas they would tend to – this when in the eighteenth century and earlier they often left these tasks to midwives. This was the case of Martha Ballard, a Hallowell, Maine midwife who attended 816 births in her twenty-seven years of midwifery – this number not including the hundreds and hundreds of people she attended to when they were ill. Scholar Laurel Thatcher Ulrich studied Ballard's diary – kept from 1785 to 1812 – and other documents associated with the town, region, inhabitants, and the few doctors who attended to people in the area. Ballard noted that when she was younger, doctors were unwilling to take on the tasks in which she engaged, but later in her life she noted that they had taken over much of what she once did, including delivering babies. It was on the frontier where midwives continued to be able to practice – where women and men relied on one another, their families, their extended kin, and their communities to survive.

Learner notes that the opportunities that had developed for women in the business and retail trades in the colonial era, and especially during the era of the American Revolution, had diminished and that there were far fewer women working in these businesses by the 1830s. For those who did continue to work in these areas, the scope of the merchandise they processed and sold changed – it came to focus almost exclusively on goods that were used by women.

Scholar Mary Ryan found in her studies that women working outside the home in Utica, New York largely did so in order to help pay for the higher education of their sons or brothers so that they could help improve the status and earning power of the family.[105] She discovered that women worked in a limited capacity and one that was focused around the home – they took in boarders, worked from within the home producing goods, and had their daughters' assistance. Ryan found that some of this work was to "consolidate as well as generate family income."[106] In Utica, New York – once a frontier itself until economic and industrial expansion changed that status – working women were really only to be found in the areas of personal service, skilled work in the garment industries, or skilled crafts. Ryan found that in 1855, of all the women in Utica, 72.7 percent were not employed, while 7.3 percent worked as domestics, 2.6 percent were professionals, 16.1 percent were employed in crafts, and 1.2 percent were found in factories.[107] Unlike Nantucket in the eighteenth and nineteenth centuries, and some maritime communities in the first half of the eighteenth century, Utica had no significant numbers of women working as entrepreneurs, white collar workers, or even shopkeepers – very few were professionals.

Alice Kessler-Harris found in her study of working women that "probably less than 5 percent of the total of married women worked outside their own homes for wages."[108] Further still, she notes that by 1860, no more than 15 percent were found in the wage labor force and this included those in industry, domestic service, teaching, and printing or bookbinding. By that date, Kessler-Harris feels that those who

48

continued to work were mainly poor. The statistics for unmarried women – both not yet married and spinsters – varied somewhat in comparison to married women. She believes that women who continued to work past the age that was believed to be more suitable for women to work especially in manufactories – teenaged years – were treated as outcasts.[109] Such limited numbers of working women who were of the merchant middle class or higher were also found in New England coastal towns, such as Gloucester and Marblehead, Massachusetts.

Maritime Communities

Gloucester, Massachusetts and Nantucket Island

Along the coast of New England, many of the maritime communities that developed in the eighteenth century as a result of fishing, trading, or whaling were located in remote and isolated spots, similar to the island of Nantucket. But unlike Nantucket, these places were not islands and they developed and grew, leaving behind their frontier status. Settled as a fishing village – a purely commercial venture to start – Gloucester was controlled locally due to its isolation. Scholar Christine Heyrman believes that "Gloucester's definitive cultural characteristics remained localism, insularity, intolerance towards outsiders, an aversion to risk, and an attachment to tradition" well into the mid-eighteenth century[110] – similar to the characteristics of Nantucket and its people in the eighteenth and nineteenth centuries.

Another parallel between Gloucester and Nantucket was the Quaker communities found within them. Perhaps because of the isolation, the Quakers found Gloucester a relatively calm place to live, where they would not face persecution. According to Heyrman,

> Because the Friends identified themselves as members of a religious fellowship that transcended geographic boundaries rather than as inhabitants of a particular town, their first loyalty was to fellow sectarians irrespective of where they resided.[111]

The Quaker religion in America was rather small and found itself part of larger communities, sometimes living quite removed from the larger community because of their religious beliefs. The fact that a Quaker community, such as at Gloucester, found refuge in another small, remote community is similar to Nantucket's Quaker community. Yet, these two communities differ because the settlement of Quakers in Gloucester was different from their settlement in Nantucket. In Gloucester, the Quakers appear to have arrived as a group from elsewhere, settling in the fishing village because they could remain alone and unscathed by persecution.

On Nantucket, the Quakers did not move to the island as a group escaping persecution or seeking refuge. They were instead already inhabitants of the island who were either practicing a religion similar to Quakerism, as Mary Coffin Starbuck was, or they were converted to Quakerism by their fellow islanders. Gloucester Quakers mixed little with non-Quaker villagers, likely as a form of self-preservation. As a result, the Quakers of Gloucester did not have a strong influence over the non-Quaker community. They neither involved themselves in political affairs nor held important political offices in the eighteenth century.[112] In comparison, Nantucket Quakers were active in local politics and held many positions of power in the community as previously noted in Part One. While separate in some cases, the Nantucket Quakers had a heavy influence over their non-Quaker neighbors in the way they lived their lives, built their homes, and established laws for the island.

Gloucester was a closed society.

> Throughout the eighteenth century, Gloucester
> did not change. In fact, its aversion to change
> recurs as the constant theme in their responses
> to the growth of a transient maritime population,
> the town's integration into an interdependent
> trading economy, their contact with larger
> seaports, and the economic success of nonnative
> entrepreneurs {evoked}a closing of their
> ranks and a determination to protect the local
> standing of their families from the inroads of change.[113]

This attitude is one that was similarly expressed on Nantucket where a suspicion of outsiders was apparent from the moment the island was settled by whites in 1659. Like Nantucket, despite the growth of the community both physically and economically, Gloucester kept its "communitarian way of life;" committed to its "corporatism" and its "localism."[114] Heyrman believes "it was because of their experience of economic interdependence, social diversity, and political contention that Gloucester's inhabitants held so tenaciously to older ways of believing and behaving."[115]

This interdependence, a community comprised of members from different walks of life and different faiths, and a focus on localism and taking care of those within the community – all aspects of a frontier – make eighteenth century Gloucester similar in many ways to eighteenth and nineteenth century Nantucket. However it was in the nineteenth century, when Gloucester was no longer considered a frontier – because the population had expanded and the economy had developed – that things began to change. This independence became lost and opportunities for women, which were available due to the social climate of eighteenth century Gloucester, began to shrink. Heyrman states that "the uneven rewards of commercial development produced a divergence of interests and values that tore apart the old corporate community" – a pattern that was found throughout New England as the frontier dissipated.[116]

Marblehead, Massachusetts and Nantucket Island

Scholar Christine Heyrman also studied eighteenth-century Marblehead, Massachusetts, another maritime community. A fairly insulated place along the coast, Marblehead, like Gloucester, was settled as a commercial venture for fishing. While today considered a charming, desirable, and expensive place to live, Marblehead was not so in the eighteenth century. It was a village with a lack of stable leadership, a lack of organized and committed religion, and a place where relationships were adversarial. All the money earned in the village went back to the businesses in Boston and Salem that had founded it. As a result, no basic institutions such as schools or local government were established, and the land was controlled by the Massachusetts Bay Colony – people were only allowed to purchase or let a small house plot with room for a small kitchen garden. With its interests in the hands of outsiders, Marblehead became a place of "assertive individualism" because people were in competition for labor and profit.[117]

It is this characteristic of individualism where one can draw a parallel to Nantucket Island. From its founding and into the first few decades of its settlement, Nantucket had no formal government. A group of elders made decisions and settled disputes. And while it was not founded by a corporation as a business venture, Nantucket was settled by a group of men seeking independence and freedom – and the governmental powers of the far distant New York Colony and later Massachusetts played little to no role on the island for many years.

Women and Work in Maritime and Quaker Communities

Because it was settled for fishing, there were a larger percentage of males than females living in Marblehead, Massachusetts. But this imbalance provided at least two advantages for women. It provided the women of Marblehead a greater choice of possible spouses and "fostered assertiveness in their dealings with men."[118] Like the wives of Nantucket's whalers, many Marblehead wives were left behind as their husbands went on frequent fishing trips. But unlike Nantucket women, Marblehead's female population tended to be aggressive towards men outside of their own families. Given the unsavory character of those who sometimes lived in and frequented maritime communities, women likely had to be aggressive in order to defend themselves, their children, and their homes. This aggressiveness likely extended to other women with whom they might have been in direct competition – whether for a man or for business.

Nantucket women tended not to be confronted with extreme individuals. Many of the island's ships put off and fitted out on Martha's Vineyard and elsewhere. The ones that did leave from and return directly to Nantucket came back to a home that carefully guarded itself from outsiders and enforced local laws to prevent as many problems as possible with outsiders. Unfortunately for the women of Marblehead, unlike their Nantucket counterparts of both the eighteenth and nineteenth centuries, Marblehead women were not as "greatly esteemed" as Nantucket women were – instead their status seemed to have been close to that of the indentured servants of seventeenth-century Virginia. Marblehead was not a family-centered settlement according to Heyrman. The status of indentured servants was not one of high esteem nor was it a family-centered system. An indentured servant was meant to work and, for the most part, refrain from starting a family. Marblehead's original settlers could have families, but their purpose was to work and make money for the businesses that created the community as a money-making enterprise.

While Nantucket women were known for their prowess for business and independence, in Gloucester, studies found only one documented instance of a working woman in the eighteenth century – a widow who stayed off the town's relief rolls by keeping the town's only tavern. She did have several counterparts in Marblehead, but only a handful of working women have been located. Most of these working women were widows who had taken over the businesses of their late husbands. Those businesses included running shops and also investing in fishing vessels. Interestingly, by the late eighteenth century, it appears that there were few working women left in Marblehead. Granted, this statistic might simply be due to a lack of recorded evidence. Perhaps with the gentrification of the town, records no longer reflected women working because it was becoming more unacceptable as the town's economy and population developed and its status as a frontier village was eradicated. The community developed into a more genteel place as the elites of the fishing companies settled in Marblehead – bringing the chaos under control and the disdain for government and religion under tighter reins, with women no longer taking over their husband's businesses. Instead, they "subsided into genteel retirement or quickly remarried" if they were widowed.[119] Some likely were also assisted by the local poorhouse, as some women on Nantucket were forced to do.

In eighteenth-century New York, Serena Zabin found that the influence of the original Dutch settlers – particularly their laws that allowed women to own property or transfer property regardless of whether or not they were married – allowed for women of different classes to be merchants, own shops, and own and run taverns and boarding houses. Zabin found that most often these women were in business for their husbands – taking over the work while their husbands were away or assuming the business if they became widows. She believes that these women did not open doors for women of the nineteenth century. Unlike Nantucket women who served as inspiration and role models for the next generations of working and achieving women, New York women did not inspire their daughters and granddaughters or perhaps even encourage them to work.

On Nantucket – although there was not necessarily a surplus of men – some widows did remarry, but often they continued on in life without their husbands. They opened or continued to run family shops or continued running their own shops that they had opened in response to their husbands going off to sea. On Nantucket in 1810, there were 379 widows.[120] This number represented twenty-three percent of all women over the age of twenty-three on an island that had a population of 6,807 – approximately three hundred of whom were free people of color, including the few surviving Wampanoag.[121] Most likely, these women were the widows of whalemen lost at sea.

Working Women in Maritime Communities in the Age of "Woman's Sphere"

It is difficult to locate maritime communities of the nineteenth century where women worked professionally – or more specifically where it is documented that women worked. There are a few instances of women working in eighteenth-century maritime communities in small numbers; however, the nineteenth century seems to reveal increasingly that women were relegated to the home or worked under the guise of women's organizations, such as benevolent societies, or as unskilled labor, such as domestics. More studies need to explore the nineteenth century and working women – particularly in maritime communities, as they were unique pockets of a variety of people, religions, occupations, and social and economic backgrounds. Again, scholars suggest that there were many instances of women working in the eighteenth century, but the act of women working declined after the American Revolution, particularly in maritime communities, because the community's frontier status was lost. Other scholars have studied places such as Newport, Rhode Island and Charleston, South Carolina and claim that changes in the Atlantic economy affected the ability of women to work.[122] The occupations they did hold in these places tended to be those that catered to the transient community – those mariners and others who came in and out of the ports on their way elsewhere looking for food, alcohol, and a place to sleep while waiting for their ship to depart. Atlantic trade in these ports depended on European connections, and such connections were lost for various reasons. The niches women filled began to disappear – mariners went to new ports and trade patterns changed during and after the Revolution. It is also important to note that unlike most maritime communities, Nantucket was and always will be an island. Maritime communities such as New London, Mystic, and Stonington (Connecticut), Marblehead and Gloucester, and Portland (Maine) are all on the mainland. No matter how isolated they were to start, they were not that far from other settlements, and then other towns and cities – there was not thirty miles of ocean between them and the nearest town. It did not take them at least eight hours by boat to get to the nearest town – and that was on a perfect sailing day.

Quaker Influences

Quaker Women at Work

Further studies concerning New York and Philadelphia – a Quaker stronghold – illustrate that women were working in the eighteenth century in large numbers. These numbers were still small, however, given the length of time studied and the fact that the study incorporated two fairly large cities. More than three hundred women retailers were found in the two cities between 1740 and 1775 – a thirty-five year span.[123] These women were shopkeepers, tavern keepers, boarding house owners, midwives or nurses, and teachers – all occupations that were consistent with the ideals of the sphere of a woman's world – the home, children, and tending to others.

Patricia Cleary's 1995 study found that these female shopkeepers tended to have only a female clientele. This coming together of women within the shop acted as a female network. Likely, it further reinforced the ideas of separate spheres that were beginning to develop towards the end of the eighteenth century. Cleary states that

> Considering women's shops as spheres of feminine
> activity, rather than simply extensions of the family,
> opens up intriguing possibilities about the meaning
> of these spaces for women. Shops may have served
> as acceptable places for women to interact in the same
> way that taverns and coffeehouses functioned as locales
> of male culture.[124]

For women of New York, Philadelphia, and elsewhere, these female-owned and run shops further reinforced the growing belief that the worlds of women and men should be separated. These female-centered shops brought women together in a sort of sisterhood, something which many scholars have noted growing as a result of women being more separated from men during the late eighteenth and nineteenth centuries.

In her work, Cleary also singles out Quaker women who were shopkeepers. However, she does not provide discussion concerning the fact that Quaker women had more support within their religious community because of the belief in equality and that this belief could extend to support women working, as it did on Nantucket Island. Also found among the female shopkeepers of Philadelphia and New York was a rivalry because they were competing for the same clients. This rivalry did not exist on Nantucket. In a small and remote geographic space with limited amounts of potential clients, the women of Nantucket tried to find their own niche and support one another so that everyone was able to support themselves through their shops and work.

Sylvia D. Hoffert's study "Female Self-Making in Mid-Nineteenth-Century America," provides a case concerning women working that may more closely resemble what was happening on Nantucket and also involves Quakers. She investigated two women who desired successful careers instead of marrying for financial security. They wanted to travel the world to locate fine silks and to sell them in Philadelphia, becoming famous silk merchants. These women were assisted in their quest by none other than Nantucket-born Quaker Lucretia Coffin Mott and Elizabeth Cady Stanton. But the help of these two women was fruitless. Even though Mott approached her Quaker son-in-law concerning the possibility of his hiring the two women to work in his silk business, in the end he refused. Societal and workplace pressures dictated that no women should be employed by his business. This was not just his decision – his partner and employees believed it was inappropriate and that to allow these two women to work with them was "taking women out of their sphere."[125]

What is most surprising is that these women were turned down by a progressive person – a Quaker – and were turned down from working among men even though there were several shops in the Philadelphia area run by women. Because these women wanted to cross into territory that was part of a male-dominated sphere, they were turned away – even by a Quaker. Hoffert believes that "Middle-class women . . . might succeed as self-made women as long as they worked within limited parameters and overcame obstacles that the lack of training, the law, and social conventions put in their way."[126] These women had attempted to cross a boundary. If they had remained within their sphere – a sphere that here included work – they might have succeeded.

These obstacles did not necessarily exist on Nantucket where women had more practical training and oftentimes better schooling than their male counterparts. Boys went to sea at a young age, but their female school companions remained at home, continuing their educations for a longer period of time. Nantucket women also had laws to support them – at least while their men were away at sea. This law was called the Mariner's Power of Attorney – a precursor to the power of attorney people use today. The wives, mothers, sisters, daughters, and friends of whalemen on Nantucket were provided with the Mariner's Power of Attorney for the entire length of a voyage. This document provided Nantucket women with legal rights that were typically denied to women elsewhere – such as the right to sell property. It is believed that between 1774 and 1847, 182 women on Nantucket exercised the right of the Mariner's Power of Attorney.

Additionally, Nantucket women lived in a society that was affected by a religion that believed in the equality of women and treated women as equals to men both socially and religiously. Furthermore, this religion affected how single women were treated within the community. On Nantucket, a single woman was treated with the same respect as a married woman. It was believed, unlike places elsewhere, that a single woman had as much to offer her community as a married woman with children. Positive treatment was also extended to widowed women who did not remarry. And, to further reinforce the acceptance of women acting outside of their sphere is the fact that women did go to sea with their husbands, although only the wives of the captain could take advantage of this privilege. Some historians have argued that being trapped within the confines of the captain's cabin or a small sunroom built expressly for the women on the deck away from the ruffian crew and their messy tasks kept women separated and still within a "home-like" atmosphere. But the simple fact that they were able to go to sea with their husbands, and that this practice started with Nantucket's whaling captains' wives in the early half of the nineteenth century, reinforces a view of Nantucket women acting independently. Some of these women acted as the ship's doctor, others as navigators, and in a few cases some stepped in when their husbands fell ill or died while at sea. Harriet Myrick Swain (1815 – 1857) was one of many Nantucket women who joined their captain husbands at sea; unfortunately, Harriet passed away from a fever she contracted while at sea with her husband in 1857. (See Appendices for a biography of Harriet Myrick Swain.)

Nantucket Island

Frontier Nantucket in the Nineteenth Century: Clan-Like, Insular, and Double-Dealing

Nantucket's status as a frontier, its independence, and, indeed, its attitude of being a separate, different, and unique place continued well into the nineteenth century. The fact that it was far at sea in an era of difficult transportation and that it had been settled by people who wanted to escape the prying eyes of government, church, and neighbors that they found on the mainland in the seventeenth century, still resonated with the descendants of these women and men. A pride of both place and being Nantucket-born and raised grew even stronger for many islanders during the era of the whalefishery. The positions of captains and officers of whaleships home-ported on Nantucket were never held by off-islanders or "coofs" – people from the outside who were not part of the extended family network of the island. These high-ranking and prestigious positions were only for Nantucketers. Nantucket whalemen were fiercely protective of this status and of their status as the finest and most successful whalemen in the world. This closing of ranks, this insulation from outsiders and the observance of a difference by using the term "coof," further emphasized the family-oriented and clan-like mentality of the islanders. It served to further foster and support the independence, isolation, and frontier status of the island both physically and mentally. Nantucket was one large corporate family economy – just about everyone on the island was related to everyone else in some way.

Nantucket's belief that it was different and set apart from the rest of America was illustrated in many other situations beyond the decks of its whaleships. The shady acts of back door deals with the British that had been an island norm during the era of the American Revolution continued with the War of 1812. Faced with a blockaded harbor and American and British ships in the waters surrounding the island, Nantucketers were cut off from supplies and communication. While it was the British who first broached the idea, Nantucketers soon found themselves consorting with America's enemy. Again, survival was the key. Nantucketers forged a deal with the British whereby certain Nantucket ships had "passports" that allowed them to transport firewood and provisions; however, this did not include fishing sloops, whaleships, or passengers.[127] The United States government had no knowledge of this "agreement." Afraid, however, that someone on island would reveal this secret deal with the British, Nantucketers soon confessed what they had done. Their confession may have also stemmed from the fact that their deal with the British was not allowing for enough supplies to come to the island. While they admitted their guilt, Nantucketers continued to make back door deals with the British – asking for the release of Nantucket prisoners and for the freedom to whale. At first, they were turned down by the British. Then, a caveat was proposed by the British. If Nantucketers did not pay taxes to the American government and officially claimed neutrality, Britain would fulfill Nantucket's requests. Nantucket claimed neutrality and the island was again free to bring necessary supplies to the island.

This attitude of being different, of having their own rights and privileges, is further exhibited in the fact that Nantucket had the first state law in America that guaranteed equal education to all students and the right of parents to sue a town for damages should their child be denied entry to school.[128] This 1845 law was likely the first civil rights bill in the United States. Granted, this was the result of a long and embroiled fight over desegregating the island's schools – resulting in riots, lawsuits, a school boycott, and petitions to the State House – because even though a Quaker ethic prevailed, segregation was still condoned and blacks were not accepted into the Society of Friends. (See biography of "Nantucket's People of Color.")

Public schools on Nantucket were fairly new when the desegregation law of 1845 came into effect. Massachusetts had established a law in 1789 requiring all towns to provide public schools. Nantucket, however, did not comply with this law until 1827, when five schools were established. Unfortunately, they were grossly under-funded because Nantucketers believed that public schools were for the poor and private schools had been the norm for many years on the island. It was not until Massachusetts forced the island to fully fund the schools via a lawsuit that the public schools became accepted. There was no public high school until 1838.[129]

Nantucket's People of Color

There was a line drawn between whites and the blacks and Wampanoag people on the island. The few Wampanoag who survived on the island – the population dwindled from approximately 2,500 in 1600 to twenty-two by 1792, with the loss attributable mainly to disease – for the most part lived with and intermarried with the growing black population on the island.[130] The Wampanoag had been ostracized over time, and their dwindling numbers reinforced this feeling. Cape Verdeans, Azoreans, Pacific Islanders, South Sea Islanders, and others who came because of whaling – as early as the 1760s – also lived with the blacks and Wampanoag.[131] Nantucket, due to whaling, became a melting pot of different cultures, and despite the segregation, there was some tolerance that allowed for these people to live on the island, even if it was just because of their ability to crew a whaleship. These people of color created their own separate world in a neighborhood known as "New Guinea." This portion of the island was past the town gates outside the official designation of "Town," where sheep and other animals were kept to graze.

Over the years, a vibrant community developed in "New Guinea" with groceries, a meetinghouse and school, boardinghouses, shops, and other businesses. By 1820, there were 274 people living in New Guinea.[132] Both men and women in New Guinea could be found working – just as with the rest of the island community. Black and Wampanoag men went to sea on board whaleships, and their wives were left behind. Interestingly, Absalom Boston, a leader in New Guinea and a mixture of both black and Wampanoag ancestry, although he identified himself with the black population of the island, was the first black whale captain on Nantucket and captained the all black-crewed whaleship the Industry. *His third wife, Hannah Cook Boston (1795 – 1857), exhibited herself to be a strong and independent Nantucket woman as well. When Absalom passed away, he left a sizeable estate, but due to an economic downturn on the island, the estate dwindled and Hannah sought other sources of income.[133] She became the first female steamship stewardess serving on board the* Island Home. *(See Appendices for a biography of Hannah Cook Boston.)*

The inhabitants of New Guinea were seen as a workforce that could be relied upon to help populate the crew of a whaleship and help to grow the island's wealth, but they continued to live separate lives despite the irony that the island was so influenced by the Quaker religion. Quakers fought against slavery. Ironically, they had few issues with segregation as illustrated by boundaried communities and segregated schools. A few slaves had been owned on Nantucket, even by Quakers before the religious sect believed in abolition, but by 1773 there were no slaves left after a court case freed the last slave on the island.[134] On board Nantucket whaleships, there was greater equality for Nantucket's black men, because crews were treated by their rank and ability not their color, but that was not the case back at home.

More research needs to be done on race relations on the island, but another area that seems to be lacking is whether and what kind of interactions there were between the women of New Guinea and the women of Nantucket town. There does not seem to be a large amount of information, nor are there primary sources available for this, but things are beginning to be unearthed by island historians. The life of one woman helps to better explain island race relations, but there are some holes. There are journals and letters missing, leaving chunks of time unaccounted for.

Anna Gardner (1816 – 1901), born and raised a Quaker, was the teacher at the African School that was housed in the African Meetinghouse in New Guinea. She was at the center of the segregation issue, as her student Eunice Ross attempted to enroll at the island's high school. Gardner, with the help of others, including Eliza Starbuck Barney, also initiated the island's first anti-slavery convention and later worked in the South establishing and teaching in schools for black children via the Freedmen's Bureau. A champion of the rights of blacks and women, Gardner returned to the island after approximately fifteen years of working for the Freedmen's Bureau and the New England Freedmen's Aid Society and helped to found Nantucket Sorosis – a chapter of the national women's group that counted numerous Nantucketers among its founders. She became known as "Black Annie" by both the island's whites and blacks. (See Appendices for a biography of Anna Gardner.)

Mary Ellen Pleasant (ca. 1814 – 1904) was a young black woman with a confusing and fairly unknown past. Little is known about her – several pieces have been written about her that are not without controversy because much of the information has skeptical sources. Her life story is made up of as many lies as truths – even her birth date is unknown and Pleasant's own limited words concerning her life are contradictory. However, Pleasant may have come to Nantucket in her early teens, supposedly taken in by a Quaker woman named Mary Hussey, a shopkeeper. Her guardian left a marked impression on Mary Ellen and may have been the first positive influence in her life, particularly as an illustration of the strength and equality of Nantucket women. Mary Ellen worked for her island years in the dry goods shop where Hussey employed several women as clerks. It is probable that Hussey's example led Pleasant to become a successful woman who not only worked as a cook and housekeeper in the boom times of the Gold Rush – often earning more than men – but also one who invested her earnings in real estate and other ventures, such as laundries and boardinghouses. Pleasant was an abolitionist, who supposedly helped to fund John Brown's Raid at Harpers Ferry and who fought for the citizenship of and equal treatment for African Americans. Much of her ability to lead and take charge, especially in business, may have been influenced by Hussey, whom Pleasant recalled in later writings about her life.

A small but still significant act of insularity and distrust of outsiders in the nineteenth century was found in Nantucket's library, the Atheneum. Established in 1834, the Atheneum kept a book in which visitors were asked to sign their names, list where they were from, and indicate who from Nantucket had introduced them to the Atheneum. Over the course of the century, many of America's (and the world's) luminaries of science, art, literature, and significant social and political movements signed this book. While a guestbook is not unusual, the fact that the Trustees and staff, in this case Maria Mitchell, asked who on the island had introduced the guest to the Atheneum is a bit different. A greater curiosity is that this book was called "The Strangers' Book" – which underscores the concept that these visitors were strangers not only to the Atheneum, but also to the island. These "strangers" were "coofs." Another point of interest in the naming of this book is that Quakers often referred to outsiders to the Quaker faith as "strangers" or "worldly" people, and this illustrates that a Quaker concept was still at play in a non-Quaker, non-religious institution – Quaker influence pervaded the island community even into the mid-nineteenth century.

An Island of Opportunity

By the late nineteenth century, Nantucket women had made an impression on the rest of the country. Close to the turn of the twentieth century, the comment was made that

> This continent could scarcely produce another
> spot whose conditions of atmosphere, of intelligence,
> of self-reliance, of thrift, would all tend to so unique
> a training, to so distinctive a life for its women as
> does Nantucket. In no other place in America is its
> womanhood so distinct, original, and independent,
> both in thought and action, as on Nantucket. This
> little island of the sea on account of its isolation,
> has preserved the strong individualism of its early
> settlers and become a community unique and
> fascinating in New England history.[135]

Nantucket women were provided with greater and more varied opportunities to work and lead than their sisters elsewhere in America.

Nantucketers varied in their economic standings, but the strong Quaker ethic that influenced all who lived on the island reinforced the belief that people should help one another – including those less fortunate. This Quaker ethic dovetailed with the beliefs that were necessary and fostered on a frontier and was further reinforced by the isolation of Nantucket. As scholar Gerda Lerner noted,

> Where class distinctions were not so great, as

on the frontier, the position of women was closer
to what it had been in colonial days; their economic
contribution was more highly valued, their
opportunities were less restricted and their positive
participation in community life was taken for granted.[136]

Lerner further states that in the colonial period the "felt inferiority of
women was constantly challenged and modified under the impact of
environment, frontier conditions and a favorable sex ratio."[137] There was
not time nor the ability to waste, debating the inferiority of a woman as
compared to a man, on a frontier where all hands were needed for
survival. Nantucket's unique situation – mainly its geographic status –
kept it a frontier well into the nineteenth century, while the rest of the
nation was evolving and changing as a society.

Whaling and Its Socio-Economic Effects on Nantucket

Island women were left alone for years as their husbands went
off in search of the whale that brought the island great wealth and world-
wide fame. The island was not bereft of men, but a large majority was
away at sea. With approximately ninety to one hundred whaleships
home-ported on Nantucket, requiring approximately twenty to twenty-
five men per ship, the island's population of 7,266 in 1820[138] was
significantly affected by this loss. In 1822, approximately two thousand
island men were employed by eighty-four whaleships and this did not
include the men who were involved with the coastal trade that boasted
approximately seventy-five ships.[139] Between 1750 and 1850, Nantucket
women outnumbered men by four to one. The island's population of
whites was approximately three thousand in 1750 and approximately ten
thousand at the peak of the whaling economy. Whaling voyages lasted
between three and five years by the early to mid-nineteenth century, as
whalemen chased the whale around the world. Thus, families were
separated for large stretches of time with only a month to a few months
at home before men returned to sea.

These men – both officers and seamen – were paid on the lay system.
Wages were not supplied during the length of the voyage. Instead, men

were paid a percentage of the sales of the whale oil and other whale by-products that was agreed to before the voyage and based upon their rank and status on the ship. Their pay day came when they returned home after three to five years. Their wives could borrow on this "lay" and take credit in local shops and with businesses on the island, but creating their own income independent from that of the whaleman was safer. It provided them with cash, allowed them to put money aside if their husbands' voyage was not successful, and assisted the wives in saving for the possibility that they could be widowed as husbands might be lost or might die at sea.

A "normal" home life was almost unknown; one woman saw her husband for only five months in the first four years of marriage. With their husbands at sea, women's responsibilities were not only to hearth and home; they had to take on what was traditionally men's work elsewhere in America and keep track of financial affairs in order to keep families from being cast into poverty. Because of this, the wives of whalers developed greater independence. They also had greater freedoms to pursue work outside the home because with men away so much, Nantucket families were small and with fewer children, women had more time to invest outside the home.

When their husbands did return home for a short break, women continued in the same manner that they had while their husbands were away. Men were not out of place in the home. On Nantucket, daily tasks continued, even the incessant visiting among women that was noted by many who visited the island in this period, including Hector St. John de Crevecoeur. The visiting was likely to keep up on local gossip, but also to help one another with physical work and the emotional toll that came with a husband at sea and little to no communication for years at a time. When their husbands were home, not only did the visiting continue, but they took their husbands along with them. As quoted in *Valiant Friend*, native Nantucketer Lucretia Coffin Mott, an abolitionist and women's rights supporter, noted that

> 'the seafaring fathers came and went; it was
> the mothers who kept the family going. For
> support of their loneliness the women turned to

each other. There was a constant visiting back
and forth on the island. When the men were
home they fitted themselves in and went along
to family teas and suppers. This seemed to
Nantucket children the natural way of doing
things . . . .'[140]

Mott stated that she knew how much of a shock such a thing would be to
people on the mainland and that for Nantucketers it would be a shock
that a separation between female and male existed. The act of visiting
and gossiping, coupled with work, has been investigated by scholars
including Nancy Cott, Karen V. Hansen, and Catherine E. Kelly, but
mainly the focus has been on lower and middling class women. On
Nantucket this was found among all classes, and all classes were affected
by whaling.

Separation and Independence Breeds Surprises and Secrets

Drug Addicts?

Little is known about the more "seedy" side of the wealthy island
nation. Down along the wharves, taverns spilled their noise and drunken
sailors onto the streets. The din from the whaleships and coastal traders
loading and unloading, and the stench from the whale oil and candle
manufactories was overwhelming. And while it was a community
greatly influenced by its Quaker religion – even after the religion began
to falter and lose favor and its island members left in large numbers for
other religions because of Quakerism's rigidity – Nantucket was not
without some problems. And perhaps it was because of the isolation and
the independent attitude that islanders, in particular a few of the women,
were found to use opium on a regular basis. Perhaps it was to handle the
stress and demands of being a woman alone trying to maintain the family
and the family's financial burdens, but during Crèvecoeur's visit even in
the latter part of the eighteenth century he noted the use of opium by
numerous women. Opium was found in the medicine chests on board the

whaleships and while scholars do not know why necessarily, opium may have been used to treat illness or other physical or mental issues.

Crèvecoeur was stunned by its use. He noted that an island physician started his day "with three grains of it every day after breakfast"[141] but that it was "much more prevailing among the women than the men."[142] He further stated

> I was greatly surprised and am really at a
> loss how to account for the original cause
> that has introduced in this primitive society
> so remarkable a fashion, or rather so
> extraordinary a want. They have adopted
> these many years the Asiatic custom of taking
> a dose of opium every morning, and so deeply
> rooted is it that they would be at a loss how to
> live without this indulgence; they would rather
> be deprived of any necessary than forego their
> favorite luxury.[143]

He was in disbelief as to why they would feel they needed to use the opium but nevertheless they did. And the continued use of opium into the nineteenth century is illustrated by the recovery of large quantities of opium bottles in the refuse left behind by the Great Fire of 1846. One can only assume that perhaps it was used for the relief of stress as noted, but it further reinforces the fact that Nantucket women were free enough that they could make these choices. Likely, many became addicts as is evident by their willingness to be "deprived of any necessary" in order to have opium. This addiction also makes one wonder if alcohol was abused, although its consumption may have been regulated to some extent, as Quakers were against its use. In the early nineteenth century on Nantucket, there were approximately sixty grog shops along the wharves.[144] Once Quakerism was no longer the force it once was on the island, temperance groups developed to combat the abuse of alcohol.

"He's-at-Homes"

In addition to the use of opium, it is believed that some island women resorted to the use of sexual aides while their husbands were away at sea. Like the purported opium use this flies in the face of the modern perception of Quaker beliefs and ways. But one has to imagine the awkward and strained relationships wives sometimes had with their husbands, at least as far as intimacy is concerned.

Often within a matter of days, weeks, or just a few months after young women married, their new husbands were off to sea for three to five years, with only a break of a few months back on dry land at home before they were off to sea again. That had to make returns – especially for newlyweds – awkward and stressful. The belief is that men likely found these aides in Asian ports and brought them back to their wives – or perhaps even their intended. While this is much more of a legend in island history, island historian Nathaniel Philbrick mentions these sexual aides in several of his works and notes that at least one was found in an island house's chimney – hidden away – along with a bottle of opium.[145] Islander and well-known editor Thomas Congdon also discussed the "he's-at-homes," as they became known, in an article in *Forbes FYI* titled "Mrs. Coffin's Consolation." Congdon's restoration of a chimney in his home revealed a "he's at home" and several empty opium bottles much to the shock and humor of him and his wife. Supposedly, other "he's-at-homes" have been found since Philbrick's publication of *In the Heart of the Sea* in 2000. Perhaps the hope was that these aides would make returns less awkward, provide pleasure, and keep their wives out of trouble. Nantucket wives were independent and did not necessarily need their husbands for pleasure.

Adultery

Even more surprising, though again not well documented, is the instance of children born out of wedlock. At least one circumstance of this in the early nineteenth century was noted on Nantucket – and there are likely more, but they had not been located at the time of this research.

Owen Chase, a whaleman who had served as first mate aboard the ill-fated *Essex*, which was wrecked by a sperm whale and was the basis of Herman Melville's *Moby-Dick*, received letters while at sea that his third wife was being less than faithful. Sixteen months after he sailed, and while he was still at sea, she gave birth to a baby boy.[146] When he returned to Nantucket, Chase divorced his wife. One has to assume that this happened more often than was ever revealed in court documents, minutes of Quaker meetings or other faiths, or in letters and diaries. The Quaker influence on the island was likely what allowed scandalous information to be kept somewhat quiet – although the Quakers were detailed in their meeting minutes about why people were disowned. But it is important to note that this air of freedom and independence did exist. A woman did not feel threatened that she would be removed from the island for a sexual transgression. It in many ways illustrates their freedom and independence. In the case of Chase, he kept the child and his former wife was removed from the island. Whalemen also had a reputation off the island but again, these are not always well documented and one wonders how many island children were fathered by someone other than the person to whom their mother was married and how many Nantucket men might have fathered children – likely unknown – in foreign places.

"Boston Marriages"

Since some or a few island women sought sexual satisfaction with a "he's-at-home" or with men other than their husbands, it seems plausible that some of these women might have sought physical or emotional intimacy with other women. Their "incessant visiting," a term first coined by Crèvecoeur in the eighteenth century, was also noted by Lucretia Coffin Mott in the nineteenth century, and the fact that many women worked so closely with one another in shops, manufactories, and dame schools, leads one to wonder whether any of these relationships grew into something more. The studies of "smashes" and of loving and sexual relationships between women that seemed to especially develop in the growing institutions for women – such as colleges and seminaries where the faculty was heavily populated by women and the students were all female[147] – leads one to draw a connection to an island that was heavily populated by women who were perhaps lonely, in need of comfort, or looking for a different sort of human companionship.

There are instances later in the nineteenth century of documented "Boston marriages" – two women living together as a couple – as have been studied by Helen Lefkowitz Horowitz and Carroll Smith-Rosenberg. While such relationships have not necessarily been obvious, the island's first female principal, Gertrude Mitchell King – the principal of the Coffin School – had a long standing relationship with Sara Winthrop Smith. Together they began a club for girls – the Goldenrod Literary and Debating Society for Girls – and small tidbits of information reveal that their close relationship lasted for decades. Another island daughter, the Reverend Phebe Coffin Hanaford (1829 – 1921), married and had two children but later separated from her husband after only a few years and began a life-long relationship with a woman. This relationship is believed to have caused Coffin Hanaford to lose one of her parishes. (See Appendices for a biography of Rev. Phebe Coffin Hanaford.) This is not to say that all Nantucket whaling wives did or may have had "smashes" or relationships with other island women that were more than just a typical friendship. It is interesting to think about what might have transpired and what might have been supported, even quietly, when such things as opium and "he's-at-homes" were in use by some whaling wives of Nantucket. These industrious women were tired, busy, likely leading stressful lives – possibly more so than their off-island counterparts – and likely needed some comfort whether it came from another individual, a drug, or a sexual aid. They were responsible for keeping the island economy thriving and their families intact while men were away at sea.

Women at Work on Nantucket

Women as Laborers

Nantucket had no real industry besides whaling, supplemented by more minor trading, fishing, and sheep farming. While there were small cottage industries such as boatbuilding or candle-making, the island relied heavily upon whaling and its support trades. With no rivers to power looms and spinning machines, Nantucket continued to live as it had in the eighteenth century and earlier. Islanders were fairly cosmopolitan and could afford luxuries and goods from off-island that were brought from around the world via the whalers and traders, but for the most part they continued to live simple lives – largely influenced by the Quaker religion – that were reflected in their laws, their dress, and even the style of their homes.

With so much of the focus on whaling, it was Nantucket's women who kept the economy afloat and who provided well for their families by running a multitude of shops – from groceries and confectioners to dry goods and shops where seamen and whalemen could purchase clothes and supplies – to working in small manufactories like the Atlantic Silk Factory and the Atlantic Straw Works. It was not a small number of women who owned shops. The recorded number of approximately one hundred does not necessarily include the women who opened shops from within their own homes or the women who did not advertise their shops. Many did not take out advertisements in the local papers – word of mouth and the fact that everyone knew everyone else helped to advertise.

Later in the nineteenth century, author and lecturer, Caroline Dall made note of what an island woman had said in regards to Nantucket's working women. Eliza Starbuck Barney (1802 – 1889) (See Appendices for a biography of Eliza Starbuck Barney) – an island force in her own right – remarked that approximately seventy women actively engaged in trade on the island. That number however, did not include teachers, the women who worked in manufactories, the women who ran shops from their homes, the women who worked for shop owners, or the women who worked in other areas, such as domestics.[148] The number of women working on Nantucket likely numbered between four and five hundred while the silk and straw manufactories were in operation. This was at a time when the island's population was approximately 8,000. Many of these women were likely part of the middle merchant class, but others came from the lower classes and also from the upper elite class. But none of the women being discussed here were domestic servants. Those did exist on the island but many of them went unaccounted for and their numbers are not included in the number put forth in this research – their numbers would swell the numbers of working women even more. No family was immune from the influence of whaling – many had husbands, fathers, or brothers who were away at sea – and this spanned all class levels.

The Atlantic Silk Company and the Atlantic Straw Company

Situated at the top of Gay Street, the Atlantic Silk Company (ca.1835) was one of several island businesses that relied upon the labor of women for its successful operation. Silk was preferred by Quakers because slave labor was not required for its manufacture, and the use of silk served as a way of boycotting cotton and protesting slavery in the American South. Unfortunately, it was likely the difficulties of cultivating silkworms on Nantucket that led to the company's closure in 1844. The building was then converted into a duplex residence that still survives today.[149]

The Atlantic Straw Company, on Main Street just beyond the Pacific Bank, also relied on women laborers during its almost twenty years of operation. Originally built as a Hicksite Friends Meeting House, the building was sold to the Nantucket Straw Loan Association for two thousand dollars on August 29, 1853.[150] The company was a subsidiary of the Union Straw Works in Foxboro, Massachusetts and was originally known as the Nantucket Straw Works or Nantucket Straw Company.[151] Advertisements were run in the local paper asking specifically for women to apply. It appears from an article in the Inquirer and Mirror *that straw works were a popular manufactory for women to work in on the mainland, and perhaps NSLA saw this as a perfect fit for the already independent-minded working women of Nantucket. This same article mentions that Nantucket women were "proverbial everywhere for their industry."[152]*

By 1854, the plant was in operation with some women working on site making hats while others worked at home. The women were given a list of twelve rules that they must follow at work. While rules were strict, a poem published in the local paper alludes to much mischief and chatter, with little work completed among the women of the Straw Company.

The Straw Company employed between two and three hundred women, many of whom may have left their children at neighborhood dame or cent schools. Cent schools – so-called because a child brought a penny a day as payment – were run by women in their homes or above shops and served working families in the community, much as day care centers do today. The schools were run on Saturdays, as well as on minor holidays, and attendance was not obligatory.[153] In the cent schools, children were taught the basics concerning reading and writing, and craft-like projects were conducted with the children, as well as art, drawing, and sewing. Many of the children returned home for lunch, but those who did not were charged an extra penny to warm their dinners. Likely, these children had mothers who were working outside of the home. Infants, pre-schoolers, and children up to the age of twelve or thirteen could be found in the cent schools. Once they were of the age for earning money or for attending the public or private schools on the island, they would leave the cent schools.[154]

By 1857, the Atlantic Straw Works had only one hundred eighty women working, and by 1858, it had closed its doors. Island women were also employed in sewing shops that fabricated products such as dusters (long coats), a manufactory that made twine, and a woolen factory. In 1811, the twine factory fabricated 23,000 pounds of twine with a value of $12,000. While men were employed by this manufactory, women comprised all of the twenty spinners.[155] The demise of all manufactories was likely due to the end of Nantucket's whaling empire and with it a decline in population.

While there were areas in which men worked where females likely did not tread, such as a blacksmith shop or a spar-making shop, who is to say that there was not a woman in the sail loft? Not everything was recorded, and there may have been a few instances of women working in these industries. While separate economies may have existed to some extent, women and men were a part of the same economy. What women did at home affected the men, and what the men did at sea affected the women back on shore. It was women who kept the economy and island life afloat while the men were away. Women provided goods and services alongside those men who were not at sea. Women maintained their family's economic and business responsibilities. The sense of obligation and dependence on one another – part of every frontier and corporate family economy – continued to exist on Nantucket despite the fact that it was the nineteenth century and that the ideas of separate worlds for women and men was a societal ideal in America. Nantucketers needed one another in order to survive. Women needed other women; women needed men; men needed the men with whom they sailed; and men needed the women at home to maintain the order, the family, and the family business and property. The fact that a street in Nantucket developed a particular female-specific nickname because of its female merchants further reinforces the fact that so many women on Nantucket were working and that work was accepted by the community.

"Petticoat Row" Nantucket

In the nineteenth century, much of Centre Street between Main and Broad streets on Nantucket became known as "Petticoat Row," because many of the businesses were owned and run by women. Women ran these businesses not only to support their families while their husbands were away at sea, but also to be prepared for the possibility of an unsuccessful voyage or the not infrequent case of their spouses' being lost at sea. "Nantucket women were, for the most part, independent out of necessity, not out of choice," according to island author and historian Nathaniel Philbrick. However, within the heavily Quaker-influenced society, women were encouraged to work for a wage, and working women were highly esteemed within the small island community. They were sometimes harassed by others – usually by men – but the community relied on their shops and the work they did in the small manufactories that developed during the late eighteenth and nineteenth centuries. They were not "feminists," although they likely influenced future women's rights activists – many of whom, like native Nantucketer Lucretia Coffin Mott, grew up with their mothers running island shops. And like the equality found at Quaker meeting, this public role gave women some leverage and social prestige.

Shops run by women were located not only on Centre Street – they could be found throughout town, many run from the front parlors of homes. The women who ran the shops – from storefront or homefront – hired other women to serve as sales clerks, apprentices, and counter help. From dry goods to confectioneries, to variety stores and grocers, women, rich and poor, managed much of the economy on the island and became known around the world for their independence and good business sense and the fact that they kept the island functioning while most of the men were away at sea. Although women elsewhere in America did work and become involved in their communities, Nantucket women were making decisions and managing finances that not only affected their families directly; they were making decisions that had a direct impact on the island's economy and its place in the world. Places such as Gloucester and Marblehead, Massachusetts boasted a few female merchants and shopkeepers in the eighteenth century, most of them widows, but they were few in number in comparison to Nantucket and began to disappear in the nineteenth century. Nantucket had a large number of shops run and/or owned by women – not all could or did advertise, so it is difficult to determine the exact number. Shops, home businesses, and shops run from homes likely numbered close to one hundred or more.

Found among the newspaper advertisements of shops owned and run by men are the advertisements of Nantucket's female-owned and run shops. One advertisement, taken out by Polly Burnell in a local paper in February 1823, lists the goods that she had recently received from the sloops Experiment *and* Enterprise. *These items included "Broadcloths, Scotch Plaids, Satins, Domestic goods of all kinds, Ready made Clothes, Beds, and live geese feathers" all of which "will be sold for cheap for cash, or exchanged for Sperm candles & oil."[156] The candles and oil were just as good as cash for Burnell and other shopkeepers – they could be sold or exchanged for other goods to be marketed in their shops.*

Caroline Dall noted the preponderance of women in business on the island in the nineteenth century in her book of 1867 titled The college, the market, and the court; Or, woman's relation to education, labor, and law. *In it, she quoted from a letter written by Nantucketer Eliza Starbuck*

Barney who said,

> *Fifty years ago all the dry-goods and groceries*
> *were kept by women, who went to Boston*
> *semi-annually {typically more often} to renew*
> *their stock. . . . Since that time I can recall near*
> *seventy women {estimated as a higher amount*
> *today} who have successfully engaged in commerce,*
> *brought up and educated large families, and retired*
> *with a competence.*[157]

Some of the women known as successful merchants and shop owners, to whom Starbuck may have been referring were: Mary Nye (See Figure 1), who decided that remaining at home was a better choice for her after spending time on board a whaleship with her husband and giving birth to several children at sea; Rachel Easton; Abby Betts; Anna Folger Coffin, the mother of Lucretia Coffin Mott; Eunice Paddock; and Mary P. and Sarah Swain.[158] *Some of the women traveled off island to stock their shops, while others relied on family and friends with sloops who could sell them goods upon arrival on the island. Some invested in whaling ships, receiving a portion of the proceeds from the sale of oil when the ships returned. Other women had large shops with diverse and extensive amounts of inventory. One woman, who was in business for more than thirty years, was said to have a shop on Old North Wharf with an inventory valued at $1,200.*[159]

Not all female shopkeepers likely had the funds or the goods to run a large downtown shop or to advertise. These smaller shops, run out of the home, relied upon selling goods to neighbors, friends, and relatives and advertising by word of mouth. Deborah Coffin Hussey Adams, a then elderly woman born in 1848 on Nantucket, recounted her childhood on the island in a handmade cloth book she made for her granddaughter. In it she stated that "we would buy tea biscuits and wonders (doughnuts) from some widow who used her 'front room' for a shop and had a bell over the front door that called her from the kitchen for a customer."[160]

This bell was a fixture over the door in many shops on the island and was captured in a poem written in the early 1920s by an individual remembering the days of the "dame-shops" clustered on Petticoat Row.

In the final stanza, the writer states,

> *Then here's to Nantucket women, /In the days of*
> *auld lang syne! /Here's to their independence /*
> *And their qualities so fine! /Here's to the wit and*
> *humor / Of many a kindly dame! /Here's to their*
> *industry and thrift, / Their honesty, their fame![161]*

Not only did the author celebrate the women who ran these shops (See Figure 2 for an image of a group of the women of "Petticoat Row"), by commenting on their independence and their ability as good saleswomen and merchants, but also the author notes that they were famous – likely beyond the shores of the island.

In her memory book, Hussey Adams further recounted that there were women's "'cent shops' all over town," which were often found in the front rooms of houses and that

> *Most of the men followed the sea going on long*
> *voyages of two and three years. They left the*
> *women to manage affairs at home. And well they*
> *did it, too. Nantucket was a 'woman's suffrage'*
> *town long before suffrage as a political issue*
> *was thought of and a notable race of women*
> *was bred there.[162]*

These women seem to have made a lasting impression on this young girl, as well as on the author of the poem, which leads one to surmise that such an impression would serve as an influence and example for young girls when they became women. The island was the home to many women who went on to serve as scientists, educators, ministers, and women's rights advocates on the national and international stage, and it was the women of Nantucket who served as their examples and as the inspirations for what these girls could do and become.

Figure 1. Mary Nye outside her shop on "Petticoat Row,"
Centre Street, Nantucket, MA, ca. 1880. F1756. *Photograph
courtesy of the Nantucket Historical Association.*

Figure 2. The Women of "Petticoat Row," Centre Street, Nantucket, MA, ca. 1860. F2879. *Photograph courtesy of the Nantucket Historical Association.*

It was natural and easy for the main consumer in the family – the female – to make the adjustment to also being the provider, particularly in an area in which a woman was familiar. These women kept the island's economy afloat while the men were away at sea. They helped support other women in their own business ventures and a distinct network of support, a sisterhood, developed. This theory of a sisterhood is a phenomenon that has been investigated by authors, such as Nancy Cott and Helen Lefkowitz Horowitz, in their analyses of women in the eighteenth and nineteenth centuries. What differs is that while the women in the studies of these two authors remained more confined to a private world where they bonded and worked together mainly in the home, the women of Nantucket were running shops and working in the public sphere together – many of them supported in their work by their husbands. It was a camaraderie, not a competition, in which each woman tried to find her own niche. On a small, remote island, they were all vying for the same customer and all trying to provide for their families, so a sisterhood of shop keepers working together was necessary for everyone's survival and for the success of the island's economy. Nantucket's unique situation of isolation, whaling, and a strong Quaker influence is what allowed island women to transcend the "woman's sphere" and work and live in the public men's sphere.

As noted, many shops were run from women's homes. A separation of the place of work from the place of residence was not found in every case of a working woman on Nantucket. Scholar Mary Ryan believes that the separation of home and place of work that occurred in the early nineteenth century is what marked the demise of the corporate family economy, an event that she claims is of "central historical importance."[163] Again, in the case of Nantucket, a different situation occurred. Men left the island in large numbers to work. Women of all walks of life and social strata took on the roles of husband and wife by providing for their families in all ways – monetarily, physically, and emotionally. Some of them worked from their homes and others worked outside the home – not just as domestic help but as shopkeepers, clerks, store owners, teachers, and in other professions in order to earn money, taking the place of the men. These women continued in their roles even when their husbands were at home, and in many cases, it seems, the husbands followed the lead of their wives. Men followed along on visits and other activities, which did happen in other New England communities, but Nantucket men allowed their wives to continue conducting businesses even when some men came home to stay permanently.

.

Conclusion: Beyond the Shores of Nantucket

*Women more than men, are bound by tradition and authority. What
the father, the brother, the doctor, and the minister have said has
been received undoubtedly. Until women throw off this reverence
for authority they will not develop. When they do this, when they
come to truth through their investigations, when doubt leads them to
discovery, the truth which they get will be theirs, and their minds
will work on and on unfettered."*

– Maria Mitchell

When Elizabeth Cady Stanton, Martha Coffin Wright, Lucretia
Coffin Mott, Jane Hunt, and Mary Ann McClintock came together for
"tea" in July 1848 to discuss what could be done for the rights of women
and gave birth to the first women's rights convention at Seneca Falls,
New York and the Declaration of Sentiments, four of the five women at
this "tea" were Quakers and two were Nantucket natives. The Coffin
sisters, who grew up in a Nantucket Quaker family, were witness to
Nantucket women managing their families and finances, running and
starting businesses, and opening their own shops for which they hired
other women to work with them. The Coffin sisters' mother opened her
own shop to support the family – first from their home and later in the
core district of the town. Often, Mrs. Coffin left for Boston alone on
business to buy goods to sell in her shop. Like other women and girls of
Nantucket, the Coffin sisters sat in pews on First Day meetings and
witnessed women standing up and speaking before Quaker meeting.
These two women did not have to "throw off a reverence for authority"
for, like Maria Mitchell, they had been raised very much as equals to
their brothers.

Whaling, the isolation, and the large Quaker influence over the island
were circumstances that helped to develop a "practical, forceful type of
woman" within the community.[164] Whether through constantly visiting

one another, or through working together in shops or church groups, sewing circles, and other social activities, Nantucket women forged many cooperative institutions of great benefit to the community. Their work and the way in which they conducted their lives would influence not only successive generations of Nantucket women and girls, but also women off island. When some members of Nantucket's younger generations, who had grown up within this unique community, left the island for other opportunities, they took these Nantucket ideals with them. They influenced others in much the same way as did Lucretia Coffin Mott and her sister Martha Coffin Wright and, also, astronomer Maria Mitchell, doctor of gynecology and homeopathy Lydia Folger Fowler (1822 – 1879) (See Appendices for a biography of Lydia Folger Fowler), and the Reverend Phebe Coffin Hanaford. They helped other women – young and old – and exemplified what women could do beyond the confines of the home and beyond what American society wanted them to do.

Nantucket serves as a strong example of how a whaling community, distant from the mainland and heavily populated for many years by Quakers, opened the doors for women to realize their potential, to be accepted in that potential by their community, and to be famous around the world. The fact that the island's people continued to act in an independent way and were physically and emotionally insulated helped to maintain a frontier mentality that allowed the men and women to continue to live as their ancestors had when they first arrived in the new land of America. Added to this was a religion that allowed for equality between the sexes and that strongly influenced other community members who were not Quakers themselves, as well as the laws of the island. Yes, there were other communities in America, particularly maritime communities that boasted populations of working women. Places such as Gloucester and Marblehead had working women and were isolated communities with economies that were fairly focused on one source of revenue. However, none seems to boast the large numbers of working women and professional working women that Nantucket did – particularly of the middle and upper classes. Furthermore, none had the unique sets of circumstances that Nantucket had – a strong Quaker influence, isolation, and an economy that relied heavily on one major source of income: whaling. Arguments abound concerning the uniqueness of Nantucket's women, but it is important to recognize that much of the research has compared Nantucket women with their counterparts in non-isolated mainland cities and ports and in communities where Quakerism was not a strong influence. Because of this, further research needs to be conducted in several areas.

The first area in need of a more thorough inquiry is the influence and role of Quaker women within their religion and their communities. At the 1987 meeting at Haverford College mentioned at the beginning, historians studying Quaker women noted that much more research had to be conducted and that they had only just begun. Further, more investigation has to be completed concerning Quaker women as workers. Out of all the women in the newly established mills and all the she-merchants of the colonial era, how many were Quakers? What kind of influence did Quakers have in other communities where they lived? How did Quakers influence other isolated communities? Secondly, what was life like for women in other isolated communities where there were no Quakers? Again, Nantucket presents a unique and unusual case study, but with limited places with which to compare it. Comparing whaling Nantucket to whaling New Bedford is difficult. Not only was New Bedford not an isolated community physically, its whaling heyday followed that of Nantucket. New Bedford and other whaling ports were located near other cities, ports, and communities, unlike Nantucket, which was far at sea in an era of still difficult transportation. And, Nantucket certainly had its own way of doing things, as has been illustrated. The islanders were not embarrassed or ashamed to do what they wanted, especially if they thought it would benefit themselves and their fellow islanders – their large and extended network of kin – their clan. It truly was an island nation.

The "nation of Nantucket" was and is not just a state of mind; it was and is a physical concept as well. The islanders felt different – and they still do – as if they were (and are) alone and fending for themselves. The fact that many islanders still term a trip to the mainland as "going to America" underscores this. Nantucket women acted as they and their mothers and grandmothers before them always had. To travel or move off island, where they were confronted with a society that frowned upon women working outside the home, was shocking and likely dismaying to them. Yes, there were women from elsewhere in America who stepped up and helped to lead the way for women's rights and the education of women and their right to work, but many of them were from Nantucket, and many more were connected to the island themselves or were close to Nantucket women.

The number of women influenced by only Maria Mitchell and Lucretia Coffin Mott is remarkable. Maria Mitchell and her students went on to influence the work of women at the Harvard College Observatory and to lead within the women's rights movement. One woman was the founder of the Home Economics movement, and one became Mitchell's successor at Vassar College as professor of astronomy and mathematics. Maria Mitchell herself was the first woman to be inducted into the American Academy of Arts and Sciences, the first female professor of astronomy in the United States, and one of the first female members of the American Philosophical Society and the American Academy of Sciences. Born and raised a Quaker and growing up on Nantucket surrounded by these powerful women, Maria Mitchell knew no differently and was shocked to see how women were treated "in America." Along with several other Nantucket women, she helped to start two organizations – the Association for the Advancement of Women and Sorosis. They were the founders of both the national chapter and local chapters of Sorosis, including on Nantucket. Several were members of the National Dress Reform Association, including Nantucket-born Charlotte Austin Joy. Austin Joy was the NDRA's founding president and, along with her husband, was active in the abolition movement and was a well-known and respected travel writer.[165]

These women were empowered by a religion, their geographic containment, the economy of a community, and by being reared in a place that respected women working in a time when many in society did not always do so. Perhaps if the mentality found on a frontier – a corporate family economy – had survived the demise of the American frontier, women would not have been put into the situation in which they found themselves beginning in the early to mid-nineteenth century.

Perhaps women would have been respected as individuals who deserved the same schooling as their male counterparts and who could work just as well.

Nantucketers needed to survive – they were alone. In order to survive, they continued to live as their ancestors did both on the American frontier in the early seventeenth century and on Nantucket in the late seventeenth century. The place in which they lived supported and nurtured women and their independence and their role as leaders and workers, who actively played a part in their religion, community, and economy. From within their churches and meetinghouses, to along the streets in front of their shops, to their government, laws and even their local newspapers that continually ran articles concerning women's rights and suffrage, Nantucket supported its daughters in their endeavors and at the same time reaped the benefits of their hard work and shone as an example of American ingenuity and success.

Nantucket women kept the economy afloat and their families safe and intact. They did not act as surrogates, just taking the place of their husbands. Rather, they acted independently and, on their own, developed their own enterprises and supported one another. Maria Mitchell once said, in reference to her family and how she was raised,

> Our want of opportunity was our opportunity –
> our privations were our privileges, our needs
> were our stimulants – we are what we are partly
> because we had little and wanted much, and it is
> hard to tell which was the more powerful factor.[166]

These words can be applied to all Nantucket people of Maria Mitchell's time and earlier, but, in particular, to the women who continued to reach and work beyond what the rest of America saw as acceptable for women. They wanted more for themselves, more for their families, more for their community. They were not afraid to do what needed to be done, and their community was not afraid to support them and benefit mutually from these endeavors.

Appendices

Introduction

Numerous women were studied during the course of this research concerning Nantucket women. While there are hundreds who will continue to remain anonymous, due mainly to the lack of information concerning their lives, there are several women who can serve as examples of Nantucket women from all walks of island life. Some of their stories are too lengthy to be included in the body of this work, but their stories merit telling and are included here within the Appendices, along with photographs. Parenthetical references have been made, as opposed to notes, with a reference list at the end of each biography.

A. Hannah Cook Boston, 1795 – 1857

First Female Steamship Stewardess

Born in Dartmouth, Massachusetts, in 1795, Hannah Cook Boston married the twice-widowed Absalom Boston in 1827, and was instantly a mother to his three children (F. R. Karttunen, pers. comm.). Absalom Boston was, of course, the well-known black captain of the all-black-crewed whaleship *Industry*, as well as a successful businessman, abolitionist, and one of the founders of the African Meetinghouse and School. Hannah was an equal partner in her marriage, just as were all Nantucket women. She became the mother of five children, helped with the creation and running of the African Meetinghouse, and supported her husband in his work of desegregating the island schools. When Absalom died in 1855, he left a sizable estate; however, in a short time, the estate dwindled to almost nothing because of the economic downturn after the Great Fire of 1846, the demise of whaling, and the Gold Rush, which lured so many away from the island.

Faced with having to find a means to support herself, Hannah looked for work outside the home. Unlike other black island women, however, Hannah did not become a domestic servant. Instead, she went to sea – following in the footsteps of her own family and her husband – by becoming the stewardess on the steamship *Island Home*. She was not serving a family, but working for the Nantucket Steamboat Company – taking care of its female passengers in the Ladies Cabin (F. R. Karttunen, pers. comm.). Hannah passed away after only a short time serving on board the steamer, but her taking this position encouraged other island women to follow suit, for several others were later employed as stewardesses on Nantucket steamships.

References

Karttunen, Frances Ruley. Personal communication.

Philbrick, Nathaniel. 1994. *Away off shore: Nantucket island and its people 1602 – 1890.* Nantucket: Mill Hill Press.

The Island Home, the ship on which Hannah Cook Boston served as stewardess.
P14276. *Photograph courtesy of the Nantucket Historical Association.*

B. Anna Gardner, 1816 – 1901

Teacher – Abolitionist – Women's Rights Advocate – Author

Born on Nantucket on January 25, 1816, Anna Gardner grew up in an abolitionist Quaker family. She was one of twelve children born to Oliver Cromwell Gardner and Hannah Macy Gardner. Her father was an ardent supporter of human rights; helping in 1822 to shield a Nantucket resident, a former runaway slave and his family, from slave catchers sent from the South to retrieve them for their former owner. While she was only six years old, this incident and her family's Quaker religion likely influenced Anna Gardner on her later path in life to fight for the rights and education of all humans – specifically blacks and women. At the age of eighteen, she began subscribing on her own to *The Liberator*, William Lloyd Garrison's anti-slavery newspaper (Anna Gardner, NHA Blue File).

At the age of twenty-two, Gardner began to teach at what became known as the African School (White 2005). She had fifty pupils in one room and taught all levels up to the ninth grade. Like Maria Mitchell and Lydia Folger Fowler, Anna Gardner had been a student of well-known island educator Cyrus Peirce, and from him she had learned and adopted his belief that memorization and strict discipline were not the keys to learning. According to Peirce, a student could be successful if she or he was instilled with a moral grounding and with a hands-on approach – learning by doing, as Maria Mitchell's and Gardner's own families believed.

Gardner's star pupil, Eunice Ross, was preparing in 1840 to take the exams that would allow her entry to the island's high school. Ross passed the exam but was denied entry because the island schools were segregated. Likely in response to this, Anna Gardner resigned her teaching position – not just in protest but to devote herself to the cause of equality for African Americans. Anna received a heart-shaped pin from her students in recognition and in honor of her quest for equal education. She would treasure this pin throughout her life, and today it is in the collection of the Nantucket Historical Association.

The following year, at the age of twenty-five, Anna Gardner initiated Nantucket's first anti-slavery convention, assisted by many other islanders including her father and her uncle Thomas Gardner. Anna served as the secretary of the organization, and the first convention, held at the Atheneum (the island's library), included speeches by many well-known abolitionists, including William Lloyd Garrison and Frederick Douglass. This Nantucket convention was Douglass' first speech to a racially mixed audience (Anna Gardner, NHA Blue File). The second convention, also organized by Anna a year later, was not as successful as the first. During the second convention, riots broke out and the convention attendees were forced to seek a safe place in order to continue their meeting. The "safe place" was a boatbuilding shop on the edge of town called the "Big Shop." It is said that men were posted outside to protect the convention goers. These riots were the result of high tensions among islanders concerning the controversies surrounding attempts to desegregate the island's schools.

Not much is known about Anna's activities after this, but in the 1860s she was one of the first people who volunteered to go into the South under the auspices of the New England Freedmen's Union Commission in order to teach in the newly created Freedmen's Schools. These schools were established under the auspices of the War Department with the assistance of the Freedmen's Bureau – part of the federal government – and private organizations (White 2005; NHA Coll. 87, Folder 2; Anna Gardner, NHA Blue File). Anna stated in a lecture she gave later in life about her experiences that the Freedmen's Commission was "guided and controlled mostly by" women and that it was the "first Society to sow the seeds of education among the freed men in that neglected vineyard of our common country" (NHA Coll. 87, Folder 2).

As she had been on Nantucket, Anna was a leader and a champion for those who could not speak or fight on their own behalf. Between 1862 and the late 1870s, Gardner taught in several Freedmen's Schools. The schools were not only poorly equipped and located in unsuitable buildings, but they were also in areas of lawlessness, where residents did not approve of a woman teacher, especially from the North, and opposed the education of blacks. At one point, she found herself living and teaching in barracks attached to a military outpost and soldiers' housing.

One of her schools in Charlottesville, Virginia had such a horrible stench that she trimmed the schoolroom with evergreen to get rid of the awful odors pervading it (NHA Coll. 87, Folder 2). Despite the poor environs, applications poured into the school, and in Charlottesville, Anna found herself with approximately eighty students, only about a dozen of whom could read. A few months later, Anna was able to take thirty of these students and form a Normal Class that she continued to teach. Another, younger, Northern woman taught the remainder of the students (NHA Coll. 87, Folder 10). Many of Anna's scholars went on to teach others; her influence and teachings reached further than she would ever know. Her perseverance and organizational abilities first exhibited, honed, and supported on Nantucket, allowed Anna to accomplish what she did in the South, even in the hostile environment in which she worked. She believed that "the school-room should be a consecrated place" (NHA Coll. 87, Folder 2), perhaps somewhat like the meetinghouse which she attended in her youth for Quaker meeting – a place where one went to await and achieve enlightenment; a place where the seed planted by God, the teacher, sprouted.

After the slaves were freed, Anna turned her attention to women's rights and to universal suffrage. In the late 1870s, Anna returned to Massachusetts where she worked with the New England Freedmen's Aid Society and where she also became active in the Association for the Advancement of Women, speaking at the Fourth Women's Congress in 1876 in Philadelphia (White 2005). Other Nantucket women, including Maria Mitchell and several of her sisters and the Reverend Phebe Coffin Hanaford, were active in the AAW, with Mitchell speaking at that same AAW meeting in 1876. Returning to Nantucket, Gardner helped to establish the Nantucket Sorosis. This women's group was first founded in New York City and boasted several Nantucket women members who were actively engaged in its national membership, including Rev. Phebe Coffin Hanaford and Maria Mitchell. Gardner served as the Nantucket chapter's secretary and president. During her time back on Nantucket, she wrote several works of poetry and the book *Harvest Gleanings* – a memoir of her teaching in the South. She lectured fairly often, many times for the AAW and Sorosis.

Anna Gardner was a woman who was well-respected and well-loved by her students and her community. "Black Annie," as she came to be known later in life on Nantucket, devoted her life to the freeing of the slaves, the education of blacks, and the promotion of women's rights. Her life was about seeking equality for others, not just for herself – something that she learned by growing up on the isolated, Quaker-influenced island of Nantucket. When she passed away on February 18, 1901 at the age of eighty-five, she left a lasting legacy, not just in the students whom she taught, but also in those her own students would teach.

References

Abbreviations

NHA – Nantucket Historical Association, Nantucket, MA.

Manuscripts

NHA Blue Files – Anna Gardner.

Gardner Family Collection. Anna Gardner. Collection 87, Folders 2 and 10. Nantucket Historical Association. Nantucket, MA.

Stackpole Collection. Anna Gardner. Collection 335, Folder 321. Nantucket Historical Association. Nantucket, MA.

Secondary Sources

White, Barbara. 1992. The integration of Nantucket public schools. *Historic Nantucket* 40, no. 3.

White, Barbara. (2005) Anna Gardner: Teacher of freedmen, "a disturber of tradition." James Bradford Ames Fellow 2004, unpublished manuscript.

Anna Gardner, ca. 1860. In this photograph, Anna Gardner is seen wearing the heart-shaped pin that was a gift to her from her pupils at the African School on Nantucket in admiration and recognition of her fight for racial equality. F190. *Photograph courtesy of the Nantucket Historical Association.*

C. Reverend Phebe Coffin Hanaford, 1829 – 1921

Minister – Author – Women's Rights Supporter

Universalist minister and author Phebe Coffin Hanaford was
born in Siasconset on Nantucket on May 6, 1829, to Phebe Ann Barnard
Coffin and Captain George Coffin, both Quakers (Hanaford 1883, 427).
Phebe's mother died when she was only six weeks old, and her father's
remarriage provided Phebe with seven half-siblings. Because she was
the oldest in a family of eight children, it is likely that Phebe learned to
lead at a young age. It is said that she often played at being a preacher
when young, mimicking what she heard from strong Quaker women at
First Day meetings. She was schooled in Nantucket and began to teach
when she was sixteen (Hanaford 1883, 427). At the age of twenty, Phebe
met and married Dr. Joseph H. Hanaford, a homeopathic physician,
medical author, and teacher in Nantucket schools. They moved to
Beverly, Massachusetts, and although they had two children – a son and
a daughter – her marriage appears to have been an unhappy one, and the
couple later separated.

At age twenty-four, Phebe Hanaford published her first antislavery book,
titled *Lucretia the Quakeress*. She would publish fourteen books in her
lifetime, including the first biography of Abraham Lincoln to be
published after his assassination. *The Life of Abraham Lincoln* sold
twenty thousand copies and was followed by perhaps her best-known
book, *The Daughters of America*, which sold sixty thousand copies.
(Hanaford 1883, 427; Tetrault 2002). This work includes essays about
prominent American women, such as Lucretia Coffin Mott, Harriet
Hosmer, Maria Mitchell, Mary Lyon, Elizabeth Peabody, Graceanna
Lewis, and Sojourner Truth – written by Hanaford and other well-known
women of the nineteenth century. The book also heavily details the lives
of Nantucket women and their influence on women around the United
States through their own work and that of organizations that they helped
to found, such as Sorosis and the Association for the Advancement of
Women. Hanaford also authored a book of poetry, *From Shore to Shore*

and Other Poems, which includes poems about Nantucket and its people, as well as *The Captive Boy* and a biography of Charles Dickens – ironic, because she was the president of the Women's Press Club that was formed in part because women were banned from a Press Club event at which Dickens spoke.

Phebe Coffin Hanaford, however, is known not only for her work as an author, but also as a minister of the Universalist Church. In 1864, she turned from her Quaker upbringing – as other Quakers later did – and studied to become a Universalist minister. She preached her first sermon in 1865 and in 1868 was ordained and asked to become the first female minister of the First Universalist Church in Hingham, Massachusetts (Tetrault 2002, 7). She was the first woman ordained as a minister in New England and the fourth in the world. She served as minister at several churches, including the First Universalist Church in New Haven, Connecticut. While in Connecticut, she was invited to be chaplain of the state legislature – the first woman in the United States and the world to officiate in a legislative body of men. Hanaford was the first woman to offer prayers for the ordination of a minister – her son – and the first woman to exchange pulpits with her own son, as well as the first woman to officiate at the marriage of her own daughter (Hanaford 1883, 428).

In a family genealogy chart that was sent out to Coffin family members, Hanaford stated, "I was the first woman ordained in Massachusetts. The first woman in the world to open a legislative session composed of men only . . . .The first woman, I suppose, to respond to a toast at a Masonic Supper. The first woman to perform the ceremony of marriage for her own daughter . . . . (NHA Coll. 38, Folder 1). She likely used a similar sermon for her daughter's marriage ceremony that she used when she officiated at other weddings – more than forty of them during her lifetime. Her marriage ceremonies were her own creation but were based upon those she witnessed as a child in Quaker meeting (Phebe Hanaford, NHA Blue File). Hanaford was obviously quite proud of her accomplishments and rightfully so. Likely, she saw herself as a leader and as an example for other women. By making note of her accomplishments, she was providing herself as an illustration of what women could accomplish, despite the difficulties they might face when confronted with the nineteenth century's belief in separate female and male spheres.

Hanaford's life was not without controversy. She remained separated from her husband for life and maintained a close friendship and relationship for forty years with a woman named Ellen E. Miles, a companionship that caused some friction in her tenure at several churches. Despite the problems, Hanaford was a popular minister with a strong following. She was a champion of equal rights for women and for African Americans and spoke from her pulpit about unequal treatment and the opportunities for change. She supported her beliefs in many other ways; for example, she always selected hymns written by women for installation ceremonies of other ministers, and she was a vice-president of the Association for the Advancement of Women, to which several Nantucket daughters belonged and had helped to found – Maria Mitchell among them. Unlike most of the women's suffrage pioneers, Hanaford lived to see the passage of the Nineteenth Amendment. She died on June 2, 1921 (Tetrault 2002, 9).

Hanaford credited much of her accomplishment to her upbringing. In a letter to the Nantucket paper, the *Inquirer and Mirror*, on March 23, 1869, she stated,

> That I have been successful as a preacher is
> largely owing to the fact of my Quaker birth,
> and my early education on the Island of Nantucket,
> where women preach and men are useful on washing
> days, and neither feel themselves out of place.
> (Phebe Hanford, NHA Blue File)

In an environment like Nantucket, it is easy to see why Hanaford and other Nantucket women both on and off the island were able to accomplish what they did. The lines of the women's sphere and the men's sphere were blurred, as the sexes on Nantucket took up the tasks commonly associated with the opposite sex elsewhere in America.

References

Abbreviations

NHA − Nantucket Historical Association, Nantucket, MA.

Manuscripts

NHA Blue Files – Phebe Hanaford.

Phebe Coffin Hanaford Collection. Collection 38. Nantucket Historical Association. Nantucket, MA.

Secondary Sources

Hanaford, Phebe A. 1883. *Daughters of America; Or, women of the century.* Augusta, Maine: True and Company.

McCleary, Helen Cartwright. 1929. Phebe Ann (Coffin) Hanaford: The 100th anniversary of her birth. *Nantucket Historical Association Proceedings* XXXV.

Tetrault, Lisa M. 2002. A paper trail: Piecing together the life of Phebe Hanaford. *Historic Nantucket* 51, no 4: 6 – 9.

Reverend Phebe Coffin Hanaford in her Vestments, ca. 1860. P15556.
Photograph courtesy of the Nantucket Historical Association.

D. Eliza Starbuck Barney, 1802 – 1889

Mother of Island Genealogy

Eliza Starbuck Barney is known almost as much for her blue H-style Victorian home at 73 Main Street on Nantucket as for her genealogical work, which is now the foundation of the genealogical collection and database at the Nantucket Historical Association's Research Library. Eliza was born on April 9, 1802, to Joseph and Sally Gardner Starbuck, the third of ten children (Stout 1998). Eliza was raised in the home of a Quaker family made wealthy by whale oil. Like other Nantucket girls who were afforded equal opportunities for schooling with those of their brothers, Eliza developed an enduring love and interest in the natural sciences, agriculture, and history. She became known on the island as a self-taught botanist and entomologist – and a good one. Her father was the Joseph Starbuck of "Three Bricks" fame, using his fortune to build three brick houses for his sons on Main Street. His daughters, he probably felt, would be provided for by their husbands.

Eliza met her match in Nathaniel Barney, ten years her senior, whom she married in May 1820 when she was just eighteen years old (Stout 1998). At Eliza's wedding, her sister Eunice met Nathaniel's cousin, silversmith William Hadwen, and within two years they were married as well. The two newlywed couples made their homes at 100 Main Street – living in two connected houses – and the two men went into business together.

Quakers and ardent supporters of the antislavery movement, the Barneys and the Hadwens welcomed many notable antislavery luminaries to their home. William Lloyd Garrison and Frederick Douglass visited 100 Main Street when they were on island in 1841 for an antislavery meeting that was organized – in large part – by Anna Gardner, with the assistance of Eliza and Nathaniel Barney (Stout 1998). Eliza and Nathaniel kept up a life-long correspondence with their cousin Lucretia Coffin Mott, frequently discussing the antislavery movement with the Motts. Several of these letters reflect Nathaniel's issue with the New Bedford Railroad, in which he held stock. For several years, Nathaniel refused to accept his dividends because the railroad would not carry black passengers – a practice that did not sit well with his antislavery beliefs (NHA Coll.178, Folder 2).

Active not only in the antislavery movement, Eliza was also a supporter of the temperance movement and involved in the equal rights and women's suffrage movements. In 1839 and 1840, Eliza served as secretary of Nantucket's Anti-Slavery Society and in 1851, with both her daughter and husband at her side, she attended the first women's suffrage convention held in Massachusetts (Stout 1998). In the late 1850s, Eliza and Nathaniel's daughter, Sarah, moved with her husband to Poughkeepsie, New York, and the Barneys followed soon after. There they lived not only in the company of their daughter and her family, but also the professors of Vassar College, including another famous island daughter – Maria Mitchell. Both the Barneys and Maria Mitchell documented these visits together.

In 1869, Nathaniel Barney died. Eliza moved back to Nantucket and within several years completed her 73 Main Street Victorian, with the help of her son Joseph. During this period of her life, Eliza served as one of two female trustees for the Nantucket Atheneum, the local library (NHA Coll. 7, Folder 12). At some point between the 1850s and 1860s, Eliza inherited the papers of the self-appointed Nantucket genealogist, Benjamin Franklin Folger (Clarke 1998). Included were the records that would form the basis of Eliza's life work: The Eliza Starbuck Barney Genealogical Record. The Barney Record, a compilation of family records and the genealogies of islanders, rests in the collection of the Nantucket Historical Association Research Library and is the cornerstone of all Nantucket genealogical research. After the death of her husband, Eliza lived on at 73 Main Street until the early 1880s, when she went to live with her son Joseph at 96 Main Street, which he had inherited from William Hadwen. In March 1889, Eliza Starbuck Barney died, leaving a priceless legacy: her genealogical records.

References

Abbreviations

NHA − Nantucket Historical Association, Nantucket, MA.

Manuscripts

Joy Family Collection. Collection 7, Folder 12 Scrapbook. Nantucket Historical Association. Nantucket, MA.

Mott Family Papers. Collection 178, Folder 2. Nantucket Historical Association. Nantucket, MA.

Secondary Sources

Clarke, Joan Elrick. 1998. The Eliza Starbuck Genealogical Record. *Historic Nantucket* 47, no 1: 8 − 9.

Stout, Kate. 1998. Who was Eliza Starbuck Barney? *Historic Nantucket* 47, no 1: 10 − 12.

Eliza Starbuck Barney, ca. 1860. F6742. *Photograph courtesy of the Nantucket Historical Association.*

73 Main Street, the home of Eliza Starbuck Barney, ca. 1870, Nantucket, MA, November 2006. *Photograph by the author.*

E. Lydia Folger Fowler, M. D., 1822 – 1879

First American-Born Woman to Receive a Medical Degree

Born on Nantucket on May 5, 1822, Lydia Folger was a descendant of famed island scientist Walter Folger Jr. and was related to Benjamin Franklin, Lucretia Coffin Mott, Maria Mitchell, and Phebe Coffin Hanaford. The daughter of Gideon and Eunice Folger, she was educated in Nantucket schools. She may have demonstrated a natural talent for science, as many in the Folger line did. This propensity for science was likely influenced further by what she learned in Nantucket schools, which at that time were still mainly private; public schools following the laws of the Commonwealth of Massachusetts were not fully instituted on the island until 1838 (White 1992). In 1838, Lydia attended Wheaton Seminary in Massachusetts and taught there from 1842 – 1844 (Dixon 1993/1994).

In 1844, she was examined by a young phrenologist named Lorenzo Fowler, who had traveled to Nantucket. During that examination, Fowler found that his subject "'not only learns from books, but from observation and experience . . . . She is also fond of natural history'" (Stern 1977, 1137). One can assume that learning from observation and experience and having a love of natural history were not just inherent in Lydia Folger, but also something that she learned on Nantucket from her teachers, family, and other islanders. The idea of learning by doing was a common way of teaching on the island. She may have been taught by island educator Cyrus Peirce, who made this philosophy the foundation of his school, and by her relative, William Mitchell, also an island educator and noted astronomer, who was the father of Maria Mitchell, America's first female astronomer. In a poem written by Lydia in 1870 titled "My Island Home," she credits the island for the education it provided her and the strong impression it left upon her, which caused her to live "with noble aims" (Dixon 1993/1994).

On September 19, 1844, Lydia Folger married Lorenzo Fowler of New York City – the young phrenologist who had examined her on Nantucket. After the birth of her first child, Lydia, encouraged by her husband, enrolled in the "eclectic" and homeopathy-focused Central Medical College in Syracuse, New York in 1849, at the age of twenty-seven (Stern 1977). At the time of her enrollment, Lydia was already well known for lectures that she gave in conjunction with her husband and for several books she had written, including *Familiar Lessons on Physiology*, a book for use by children. It was her Nantucket cousin, Lucretia Coffin Mott, who helped Lydia gain access to the school (Dixon 1993/1994). The year 1849 was the same year that Elizabeth Blackwell received her medical degree, making her America's first female physician. Lydia was one of three female students enrolled in the college, and when she graduated in 1850, she was the only female graduate. While Blackwell claimed fame as the first American woman to graduate from medical school, Lydia could claim that she was the first American-born woman to earn a medical degree.

Just two months after graduating, Lydia gave birth to her second child. In that same year, she was appointed by the college as the Principal of the Female Department and the demonstrator of anatomy for female students (Stern 1977). While women were allowed into the college, and they had the same course of study as men, some of the classes were separated – anatomy in particular – because it was believed to be inappropriate for women and men to take these classes together. Later, Lydia was appointed as the Professor of Midwifery and Diseases of Women and Children at the college (Stern 1977). Lydia's position as professor at the medical college made her the first female professor of medicine in the United States. In 1851, Lydia became the first female physician in the United States to address an organized society of medical men. In 1852, after several years of conflict, which included the college's move to Rochester, New York, it finally closed. Lydia then opened her own practice in New York City at 50 Morton Street with a focus in gynecology. She could also be found in the late afternoons practicing in her husband's phrenology offices (Stern 1977).

With a private practice and no students or class schedules to keep, Lydia began to tour with her husband on the lecture circuit – both of them providing lectures around the country and throughout Europe. Lydia's audience was female, and she lectured on the physiology and diseases of women and, later, on the effects of alcohol on physiology. She noted in an undated letter to her brother, Allen Folger, living in Gardner, Massachusetts, that it was difficult to leave behind her three daughters for the European trip, but that she felt that it was "for their good and happiness" (NHA Coll. 118, Folder 37). She was away for at least a year. In this same letter, the only one that is in the collection at the Nantucket Historical Association, she referred to a man, possibly the manager or scheduler of the husband and wife duo, who gave her some difficulty over speaking engagements so she "keep{s} quiet or {she would} be in hot water all the time" (NHA Coll. 118, Folder 37). Perhaps her limited engagements to female-only audiences were the doings of this gentleman to whom she refers.

During this period, Lydia became associated "with two other institutions, both of an unconventional nature" (Stern 1977, 1138). These were the New York Hydropathic and Physiological School and the Metropolitan Medical School. At the first school, Lorenzo also lectured. Lydia lectured on midwifery and female diseases. Much of the Hydropathic School was focused on the healing powers of cold water, hard mattresses, and graham bread, which dovetailed with some of the beliefs of the temperance movement – something in which Lydia also actively participated.

Lydia and Lorenzo continued to lecture around the country and then in Europe, where Lorenzo opened a branch of his phrenology office in London. It was here that Lydia furthered her work by publishing more of her lectures, becoming an active member of the British Women's Temperance Association, and serving the poor of London's and Ireland's slums whom she visited to dispense medical treatment, birth babies, and provide assistance and information concerning hygiene (Dixon 1993/1994). Ironically, it was from those she was helping that Lydia contracted a disease that became pleuropneumonia. She passed away on January 26, 1879, having lived her professional life attempting to determine the cause of diseases and effective treatments for them, particularly among women and children.

"My Island Home" by Lydia Folger Fowler, originally published in *Heart Melodies*, a book of poetry published in 1870. Taken from Alice Dixon's article in *Historic Nantucket*.

For every island child can learn
to write, and spell, and read
Without expense in public schools
that are good schools indeed.
In literary attainments
that island of the sea
Is the Athens of the region,
long may it ever be.
Its sons and daughters may depart
and travel o'er the earth
Their Island Home they'll not forget,
the isle that gave them birth.
As the native soil is fertile
in which the acorn lies,
So will grow the umbrageous oak
with branches to the skies.
As is the earliest bias
that the young child receives,
So will an influence be given
that never, never leaves
That child: where'er his destiny
may send him forth to roam
His heart will ever bear the seal
stamped at his childhood's home.
If I have led a useful life,
and good to others done,
If I have lived with noble aims,
the motive power has come
From strong impress I received
at my dear island home
Before I ever ventured forth
in the wide world to roam.
As children think with gratitude
of mothers very kind
Who hold them by the cords of love
which they know how to bind,
So of that isle I love to think,
that isle beyond the sea,
For the memory of that isle
is very dear to me.

References

Abbreviations

NHA – Nantucket Historical Association, Nantucket, MA.

Manuscripts

Folger Family Collection. Collection 118, Folder 37. Nantucket Historical Association. Nantucket, MA.

Stackpole Collection. Collection 335, Folder 307. Nantucket Historical Association. Nantucket, MA.

Secondary Sources

Dixon, Alice. 1993/1994. A lesser-known daughter of Nantucket: Lydia Folger Fowler. *Historic Nantucket* 41: no. 4 60-62.

Hanaford, Phebe A. 1883. *Daughters of America; Or, women of the century.* Augusta, Maine: True and Company.

Stern, Madeleine B. Lydia Folger Fowler: *First American woman professor of medicine. New York State Journal of Medicine* (June *1977*).

White, Barbara. The integration of Nantucket public schools. *Historic Nantucket* 40, no. 3 (Fall 1992).

Lydia Folger Fowler, ca. 1860. F900. *Image courtesy of the Nantucket Historical Association.*

F. Harriet Myrick Swain, 1815 – 1857

Woman on Board

Harriet Myrick Swain was one of several Nantucket women to join their husbands at sea. Swain and her husband, Captain Obed Swain, sailed on board the *Catawba* on Christmas Day 1852 for what would become a three-year voyage. Harriet chose to join her husband rather than spend three to five years of separation, which many whaling couples endured. Going to sea, however, was an option only for the captain's wife. Obed had a small room built for her on the deck so that she could enjoy the sea air and be outside without risking sunburn. During the journey, Harriet kept a journal of her experiences on board. She recorded the daily monotony, bouts of seasickness, whales caught, and the loss of crew members. One incident that particularly affected her was the loss of a nineteen-year-old boy whom she memorialized with a poem. Harriet did not complete the journey; she became ill and was put ashore at Payta, Peru to be sent home. She recounted all of this in her journal. Unfortunately, although she made it home safely, Harriet passed away from a fever just twenty-one days before Obed returned home in 1857.

References

Abbreviations

NHA – Nantucket Historical Association, Nantucket, MA.

Manuscripts

Ships Log Collection. Collection 220, Log 33. Nantucket Historical Association. Nantucket, MA.

Notes

[1]Mary P. Ryan, *Cradle of the Middle Class: The Family in Oneida County, New York, 1790 – 1865* (Cambridge: Cambridge University Press, 1981), 19.

[2] Ibid., 231.

[3] Ibid., 22.

[4]Sara M. Evans, *Born for Liberty: A History of Women in America* (New York: Free Press Paperbacks, 1997), 28.

[5] Ibid., 28.

[6] Ibid., 28.

[7] Ryan, 41.

[8] Ibid., 41.

[9] Ibid., 41.

[10]Karen V. Hansen, *A Very Social Time: Crafting Community in Antebellum New England* (Berkeley: University of California Press, 1994).

[11] Ryan, 43.

[12] Ibid., 25.

[13] Evans.

[14] Ibid., 36.

[15] Ibid., 35.

[16] Alice Kessler-Harris, *Out to Work: A History of Wage-Earning Women in the United States* (Oxford: Oxford University Press, 2003).

[17]Nathaniel Philbrick, *Away Off Shore: Nantucket Island and Its People 1602 – 1890* (Nantucket: Mill Hill Press, 1994).

[18]Edward Byers, *The Nation of Nantucket: Society and Politics in an Early American Commercial Center, 1660 – 1820* (St. Petersburg, Florida: Hailer Publishing, 1987), 35.

[19] Ibid., 35.

[20] Ryan, 20.

[21] Byers.

[22] Ibid., 47.

[23]Hector St. John de Crèvecoeur, *Letters from an American Farmer and Sketches of Eighteenth-Century America* (1782; reprint Penguin Books, New

York, 1998), 153.

[24] Byers, 329.

[25] Ibid., 48.

[26] Ibid., 51.

[27] Philbrick, 1994.

[28] Rufus Jones, Isaac Sharpless, Amelia Gummere, *The Quakers in the American Colonies* (London: MacMillan and Co., Limited, 1911), xvii.

[29] Robert Leach, Peter Gow, *Quaker Nantucket: The Religious Community Behind the Whaling Empire* (Nantucket: Mill Hill Press, 1997), 26.

[30] Thomas Hamm, *The Quakers in America* (New York: Columbia University Press, 2003), 18.

[31] William J. Frost, *The Quaker Family in Colonial America* (New York: St. Martin's Press, 1973), 15.

[32] Byers, 109.

[33] Hamm, 21.

[34] Byers, Hamm, Leach and Gow.

[35] Kessler-Harris, 15.

[36] Hamm, 22.

[37] Ibid.

[38] Ibid., 22.

[39] Hamm, 22.

[40] Mary Maples Dunn, "Saints and Sisters: Congregational and Quaker Women in the Early Colonial Period," *American Quarterly* 30:5 (Winter 1978) http://www.jstor.org/stable/2712399, 583.

[41] Ibid.

[42] Ibid., 584.

[43] Ibid., 596.

[44] Ibid., 596.

[45] Hussey Family Papers. Christopher Adams Collection. Collection 321, Folder 3. NHA.

[46] Jones, Sharpless, and Gummere, 124.

[47] Leach and Gow, 26.

[48] Philbrick 1994, 78-9.

[49] R. A. Douglas-Lithgow, *Nantucket: A History* (New York: G. P. Putnam's Sons, 1914), 119.

[50] Byers, 103.

[51] Leach and Gow, 27.

[52] Byers, 53.

[53] Lisa Norling, *Captain Ahab Had a Wife: New England Women and the Whalefishery, 1720 – 1870* (Chapel Hill: The University of North Carolina Press, 2000), 57.

[54] Leach and Gow, 27.

[55] Byers, 329.

[56] Nantucket Monthly Meeting of Friends Membership (1708 – 1876). Collection 52, Book 20. NHA.

[57] Obed Macy, *The History of Nantucket; Being a Compendious Account of the First Settlement on the Island by the English, Together with the Rise and Progress of the Whale Fishery; and Other Historical Facts Relative to Said Island and its Inhabitants* (Boston: Hilliard, Gray, and Co., 1835), 36.

[58] Leach and Gow, 28.

[59] NHA Coll. 52, Bk. 10, 1.

[60] Byers.

[61] Ibid., 33.

[62] Leach and Gow.

[63] Byers, 53.

[64] Ibid., 105.

[65] Ibid., 108.

[66] Ibid., 107.

[67] Crèvecoeur, 156.

[68] Ibid., 148.

[69] Leach and Gow, 25.

[70] Byers, 108.

[71] Byers, 329; Leach and Gow, 44.

[72] Byers, 329; Leach and Gow, 35.

[73] Byers, 136.

[74] Ibid., 321.

[75] Leach and Gow, 81.

[76] Crèvecoeur, 110-111.

[77] Ibid., 155.

[78] Byers, 175.

[79] NHA Coll. 52, Bk. 10, 76.

[80] Leach and Gow, 104.

[81] Ibid.

[82] Philbrick, 1994, 126.

[83] Crèvecoeur, 109.

[84] Byers, 329.

[85] Byers, 178; Frost, 70.

[86] Byers, 178.

[87] Crèvecoeur, 159.

[88] Margaret Moore Booker, "Woman's Sphere": Women in the Arts on Nantucket, 1795 – 1945 in Michael A. Jehle, ed., *Picturing Nantucket: An Art History of the Island with Paintings from the Collection of the Nantucket Historical Association*, (Nantucket: Nantucket Historical Association, 2000), 49-68.

[89] Byers, 329.

[90] Ibid., 210-211.

[91] Stevens, 99.

[92] Rotch Family Papers. Collection 101, Folder 3. NHA.

[93] Ibid.

[94] Stevens, 101.

[95] Evans, 46-7.

[96] Crèvecoeur, 157.

[97] Maria Mitchell Papers. Box 22, Folder 1. MMA.

[98] Lisa Norling, "Judith Macy and her Daybook; or Crèvecoeur and the Wives of Sherborn," *Historic Nantucket* 40:4 (1992), 69.

[99] Account Books. Collection10, AB 37 C1. NHA.

[100] Elizabeth Cady Stanton, Susan B. Anthony, Matilda Joslyn Gage, eds, *History of Woman Suffrage, Volume I, 1848 – 1861* (New York: Charles Mann, 1887), 407-408.

[101] Crèvecoeur, 108.

[102] Stevens, 92.

[103] Barbara Welter, "The Cult of True Womanhood: 1820 – 1860," *American Quarterly* 18:2 (Summer 1966) http://wwjstor.org/stable/2711179.

[104] Gerda Lerner, "The Lady and the Mill Girl: Changes in the Status of Women in the Age of Jackson," *American Studies* 10:1 (Spring 1969): 7.

[105] Ryan, 172.

[106] Ibid., 201.

[107] Ibid., 274.

[108] Kessler-Harris, 46.

[109] Ibid., 53.

[110] Christine Leigh Heyrman, *Commerce and Culture: The Maritime Communities of Colonial Massachusetts, 1690 – 1750* (New York: W. W. Norton and Company, 1984), 143.

[111] Ibid., 139.

[112] Ibid., 9.

[113] Ibid., 168.

[114] Ibid., 204.

[115] Ibid., 204.

[116] Ibid., 28.

[117] Ibid., 241.

[118] Ibid., 216.

[119] Ibid., 382.

[120] Byers, 257.

[121] Ibid., 329.

[122] Ellen Hartigan-O'Connor, "'She Said She Did Not Know Money': Urban Women and Atlantic Markets in the Revolutionary Era," *Early American Studies: An Interdisciplinary Journal* 4:2 (Fall 2006).

[123] Patricia Cleary, "'She Will Be in the Shop': Women's Sphere of Trade in Eighteenth-Century Philadelphia and New York," *The Pennsylvania Magazine of History and Biography* 119:3 (July 1995), 183 (http://www.psu.pmhb/1205256668).

[124] Ibid., 200.

[125] Sylvia D Hoffert, "Female Self-Making in Mid-Nineteenth Century America," *Journal of Women's History* 120: 3 (Fall 2008): 40.

[126] Ibid., 38.

[127] Macy, 195.

[128] Barbara White, "Anna Gardner: Teacher of Freedmen, 'A Disturber of Peace.'" Paper presented in 2005 as a James Bradford Ames Fellow.

[129] Barbara White, "The Integration of Nantucket Public Schools," *Historic Nantucket* 40:3 (1992), 59 - 62.

[130] Byer, 329.

[131] Philbrick, 1994, 179.

[132] Ibid.

[133] Frances Ruley Karttunen, Ph.D, personal communication regarding her

research on Hannah Cook Boston.

[134] Philbrick, 1994, 178.

[135] Aaron Merritt Hill, *Life and Labors of Mrs. Mary A. Woodbridge* (Ravenna, Ohio: F. W. Woodbridge, 1895), Harvard University Library, Women Working Website 1800-1930, 29-30.

[136] Lerner, 12.

[137] Ibid., 7.

[138] Byers, 329.

[139] Byers, 296.

[140] Margaret Hope Bacon, *Valiant friend: The life of Lucretia Mott* (New York: Walker and Company, 1980), 17.

[141] Crèvecoeur, 160.

[142] Ibid.

[143] Ibid., 160.

[144] Philbrick, 1994.

[145] Nathaniel Philbrick, *In the Heart of the Sea: The Tragedy of the Whaleship Essex* (New York: Viking, 2000).

[146] Ibid., 216.

[147] Helen Lefkowitz Horowitz, *The Power and Passion of M. Carey Thomas* (New York: Alfred A. Knopf, 1994). Carroll Smith-Rosenberg, *Disorderly Conduct: Visions of Gender in Victorian America* (New York: Oxford University Press, 1986).

[148] Caroline H. Dall, *The College, the Market, and the Court; Or, Woman's Relation to Education, Labor, and Law* (Boston: Lee and Shepard, 1867), 197-198.

[149] Clay Lancaster, *The Architecture of Historic Nantucket* (New York: McGraw-Hill Book Company, 1972).

[150] Preservation Institute: Nantucket, "Atlantic Straw Works," Preservation Institute: Nantucket, 1996-92.

[151] Ibid.

[152] Ibid.

[153] Cent Schools, NHA Blue Files.

[154] Ibid.

[155] Byers.

[156] Business and Industry, NHA Blue File.
[157] Dall, 198.
[158] Phebe A.Hanaford, *Daughters of America; Or, Women of the Century* (Augusta, Maine: True and Company, 1883).

[159] Diane Ucci, "Whaling Voyages and Quaker Ideals: Creation of the Nantucket Women's Working Force, *Nantucket Guide* (1991), NHA "Business and Industry" Blue File.

[160] Coll. 321, Folder 3. NHA.
[161] Petticoat Row, NHA Blue File.
[162] NHA Coll. 321, Folder 3.
[163] Ryan, 231.
[164] Stevens, 94.
[165] Joy Family Collection. Coll.7, Folder 12. NHA.
[166] Maria Mitchell Papers. Box 3, Folder 11. MMA.

References

Abbreviations

MMA – Nantucket Maria Mitchell Association, Nantucket, MA.

NHA – Nantucket Historical Association, Nantucket, MA.

Manuscripts

MMA:

Maria Mitchell Papers. Box 1, Folder 2. MMA.

Maria Mitchell Papers. Box 2, Folder 1. MMA.

Maria Mitchell Papers. Box 3, Folder 11. MMA.

Scrapbook of M. Florence Easton. Box 22, Folder 1. MMA.

NHA:

Account Book Collection. Collection 10, AB 37-C1. NHA.

Kezia Coffin Fanning Papers (1775 – 1820). Collection 2. NHA.

Folger Family Collection. Collection 118, Folder 37. NHA.

Gardner Family Collection. Anna Gardner. Collection 87, Folders 2 and 10. NHA.

Phebe Coffin Hanaford Collection. Collection 38. NHA.

Hussey Family Papers. Christopher Adams Collection. Collection 321, Folder 3. NHA.

Joy Family Collection. Collection 7, Folder 12 Scrapbook. NHA.

Macy Family Papers. Collection 96, Folder 3.75. NHA.

Mott Family Papers. Collection 178, Folder 2. NHA.

Nantucket Monthly Meeting of Friends (1708 – 1787). Collection 51. NHA.

Nantucket Monthly Meeting of Friends Membership (1708 – 1876). Collection 52, Book 20. NHA.

Nantucket Women's Meeting (1708 – 1787). Collection 52, Book 10. NHA.

Nantucket Schools Collection (1788 – 1980). Collection 88. NHA.

Rotch Family Papers. Collection 101, Folder 3. NHA.

Ships Log Collection. Collection 220, Log 33. NHA.

Ships Log Collection. Collection 220, Log 136. NHA.

Stackpole Collection. Collection 335, Folder 307. NHA.

Stackpole Collection. Anna Gardner. Collection 335, Folder 321. NHA.

NHA Blue Files:

Anna Gardner

Business and Industry, files 1, 2, and 3

Cent Schools

Petticoat Row

Phebe Hanaford

Quakers

Sorosis

Women

Nantucket Atheneum:

"The Book of Strangers" also referred to as "The Visitors Book: Strangers Introduced to the Nantucket Atheneum" collection of guest books, nineteenth and early twentieth century.

Published Primary Sources

Crevecoeur, Hector St. John de. 1782/1998. *Letters from an American farmer and sketches of eighteenth-century America.* Ed. and intro by Albert E. Stone. New York: Penguin Books.

Dall, Caroline H. 1867. *The college, the market, and the court; Or, woman's relation to education, labor, and law.* Boston: Lee and Shepard.

Fuller, Margaret. *Woman in the nineteenth century.* 1971. New York: W.W. Norton and Company.

Hanaford, Phebe A. 1883. *Daughters of America; Or, women of the century.* Augusta, Maine: True and Company.

Howe, Julia Ward. 1899. *Reminiscences: 1819 – 1899.* Boston: Houghton, Mifflin, and Company.

Kendall, Phebe Mitchell, ed. 1896. *Maria Mitchell: Life, letters, and journals*. Boston: Lee and Shepard Publishers.

Macy, Obed. 1835. *The history of Nantucket; Being a compendious account of the first settlement on the island by the English, together with the rise and progress of the whale fishery; and other historical facts relative to said island and its inhabitants.* Boston: Hilliard, Gray, and Co.

Secondary Sources

Maritime Women and Maritime Communities

Druett, Joan, ed. 1992. *'She was a sister sailor': The whaling journals of Mary Brewster, 1845 – 1851*. Mystic, Connecticut: Mystic Seaport Museum.

Hartigan-O'Connor, Ellen. 'She said she did not know money': Urban women and Atlantic markets in the revolutionary era. *Early American Studies: An Interdisciplinary Journal* 4, no. 2 (Fall 2006). http://muse.jhu.edu/journals/early_american_studies_an_interdisci plinary_journal (accessed April 1, 2009).

Heyrman, Christine Leigh. 1984. *Commerce and culture: The maritime communities of colonial Massachusetts, 1690 – 1750*. New York: W. W. Norton and Company.

Norling, Lisa. 2000. *Captain Ahab had a wife: New England women and the whalefishery, 1720 – 1870*. Chapel Hill: The University of North Carolina Press.

Nantucket Sources

Albers, Henry, ed. 2001. *Maria Mitchell: A life in journals and letters.* Clinton Corners, New York: College Avenue Press.

Bergland, Renee. 2008. *Maria Mitchell and the sexing of science: An astronomer among the American romantics.* Boston: Beacon Press.

Booker, Margaret Moore. 2007. *Among the stars: The life of Maria Mitchell.* Nantucket: Mill Hill Press.

———. 2000. "Woman's sphere": Women in the arts on Nantucket, 1795 – 1945. In *Picturing Nantucket: An art history of the island with paintings from the collection of the Nantucket Historical Association,* ed. Michael A. Jehle, 49–68. Nantucket: Nantucket Historical Association.

———. 2001. *Nantucket spirit: The art and life of Elizabeth Rebecca Coffin.* Nantucket: Mill Hill Press.

———. 1998. *The admiral's academy: Nantucket Island's historic Coffin School.* Nantucket: Mill Hill Press.

Byers, Edward. 1987. *The nation of Nantucket: Society and politics in an early American commercial center, 1660 – 1820.* St. Petersburg, Florida: Hailer Publishing.

Coffin, Eliza G. "The Woman's Sphere." *Inquirer and Mirror,* May 9, 1874.

Congdon, Thomas. 1997. Mrs. Coffin's consolation. *Forbes FYI,* Fall.

Douglas-Lithgow, R. A. 1914. *Nantucket: A history.* New York:

G. P. Putnam's Sons.

Hart, Joseph. 1834/1995. *Miriam Coffin, or the whale-fishermen.* Nantucket: Mill Hill Press.

Lancaster, Clay. 1972. *The Architecture of Historic Nantucket.* New York: McGraw-Hill Book Company.

Leach, Robert and Peter Gow. 1997. *Quaker Nantucket: The religious community behind the whaling empire.* Nantucket: Mill Hill Press.

McCleary, Helen Cartwright. 1929. Phebe Ann (Coffin) Hanaford: The 100th anniversary of her birth. *Nantucket Historical Association Proceedings* XXXV.

Macy, William F. 1930. *The Nantucket scrap basket: Being a collection of characteristic stories and sayings of the people of the town and island of Nantucket, Massachusetts.* 2nd ed. Boston: Houghton Mifflin Company.

Norling, Lisa. 1992. Judith Macy and her daybook; or Crèvecoeur and the wives of Sherborn. *Historic Nantucket* 40, no 4: 68 – 71.

Philbrick, Nathaniel. 2000. *In the heart of the sea: The tragedy of the whaleship* Essex. New York: Viking..

———. 1994. *Away off shore: Nantucket island and its people 1602 – 1890.* Nantucket: Mill Hill Press.

———. 1991. The Nantucket sequence in Crevecoeur's letters from an American farmer. *The New England Quarterly* 64, no. 3 (Sep. 1991). http://www.jstor.org/stable/366350 (accessed October 23, 2008).

Preservation Institute: Nantucket. 1996. Atlantic Straw Works.

Preservation Institute: Nantucket, 1996-92.

Stevens, William Oliver. 1936. *Nantucket: The far-away island.* New York: Dodd, Mead, and Company.

Quaker

Brown, Elisabeth Potts and Susan Mosher Stuard, eds. 1989. *Witnesses for change: Quaker women over three centuries.* New Brunswick, New Jersey: Rutgers University Press.

Dunn, Mary Maples. Saints and sisters: Congregational and Quaker women in the early colonial period. *American Quarterly* 30, no.5 (Winter 1978). http://www.jstor.org/stable/2712399 (accessed November 24, 2008).

Frost, J. William. 1973. *The Quaker family in colonial America.* New York: St. Martin's Press.

Hamm, Thomas. 2003. *The Quakers in America.* New York: Columbia University Press.

Hamm, Thomas. Quakerism, ministry, marriage, and divorce: The ordeal of Priscilla Hunt Cadwalader. *Journal of the Early Republic* 28, no.3 (Fall 2008). http://muse.jhu.edu/journals/journal_of_the_early_republic/v028/2 8.3.hamm.html   (accessed April 1, 2009).

Jones, Rufus, Isaac Sharpless and Amelia Gummere. 1911. *The Quakers in the American colonies.* London: MacMillan and Co., Limited.

Tomes, Nancy. 1982. The Quaker connection: Visiting patterns among women in the Philadelphia Society of Friends, 1750 – 1800.

In *Friends and neighbors: Group life in America's first plural society.* ed. Michael Zuckerman, 174 - 195. Philadelphia: Temple University Press.

Women's History and Gender Studies

Bacon, Margaret Hope. 1980. *Valiant friend: The life of Lucretia Mott.* New York: Walker and Company.

Cleary, Patricia. 'She will be in the shop': Women's sphere of trade in eighteenth-century Philadelphia and New York. *The Pennsylvania Magazine of History and Biography* 119, no. 3 (July 1995). http://www.psu.pmhb/1205256668 (accessed April 28, 2009).

Cott, Nancy. 1977. *The bonds of womanhood: 'Woman's sphere' in New England, 1780 –1835.* New Haven: Yale University Press.

———, ed. 1972. *The root of bitterness: Documents of the social history of American women.* New York: E. P. Dutton and Co., Inc.

Creighton, Margaret S. and Lisa Norling, eds. 1996. *Iron men, wooden women: Gender and seafaring in the Atlantic world, 1700 – 1920.* Baltimore: Johns Hopkins University Press.

Dublin, Thomas. 1979. *Women at work: The transformation of work and community in Lowell, Massachusetts, 1826 – 1860.* New York: Columbia University Press.

Evans, Sara M. 1997. *Born for liberty: A history of women in America.* New York: Free Press Paperbacks.

Ginzberg, Lori D. 1990. *Women and the work of benevolence: Morality, politics, and class in the nineteenth-century United*

States. New Haven: Yale University Press.

Hansen, Karen V. 'No Kisses is Like Youres': An erotic friendship between two African-American women during the mid-nineteenth century. *Gender & History* 7, no.2 (August 1995).

———. 1994. *A very social time: Crafting community in antebellum New England*. Berkeley: University of California Press.

Hill, Aaron Merritt. 1895. *Life and labors of Mrs. Mary A. Woodbridge*. Ravenna, Ohio: F. W. Woodbridge. Harvard University Library, Women Working Website 1800-1930. http://nrs.harvard.edu/urn-3:FHCL:479101. (accessed March 2009).

Hoffert, Sylvia D. Female self-making in mid-nineteenth century America. *Journal of Women's History* 120, no. 3 (Fall 2008). http://muse.jhu.edu/journals/journal_of_womens_history/v020/20.3.hoffert.html (accessed April 1, 2009).

Horowitz, Helen Lefkowitz. 1994. *The power and passion of M. Carey Thomas*. New York: Alfred A. Knopf.

———. 1984. *Alma mater: Design and experience in the women's colleges from their nineteenth-century beginnings to the 1930s*. New York: Alfred A. Knopf, Inc.

Kelly, Catherine E. 1999. *In the New England fashion: Reshaping women's lives in the nineteenth century*. Ithaca: Cornell University Press.

Kerber, Linda. Separate spheres, female worlds, woman's place: The rhetoric of women's history. *The Journal of American History* 75, no. 1 (June 1988). http://www.jstor.org/stable/1889653 (accessed November 11, 2008).

Kessler-Harris, Alice. 2003. *Out to work: A history of wage-earning women in the United States*. Oxford: Oxford University Press.

Lerner, Gerda. The lady and the mill girl: Changes in the status of women in the age of Jackson. *American Studies* 10, vol. 1 (Spring 1969). https://journals.ku.edu/index.php/amerstud/article/viewfile/2145/2104 (accessed March 25, 2009).

Macdonald, Cameron Lynne and Karen V. Hansen. Sociability and gendered spheres: visiting patterns in nineteenth-century New England. *Social Science History* 25, no. 4 (Winter 2001). http://muse.jhu.edu/journals/social_science_history/v025/25.4macdonald.html (accessed April 1, 2009).

Nylander, Jane. 1993. *Our own snug fireside: Images of the New England home, 1760 – 1860*. New Haven: Yale University Press.

Ryan, Mary P. 1981. *Cradle of the middle class: The family in Oneida County, New York, 1790 – 1865*. Cambridge: Cambridge University Press.

Smith-Rosenberg, Carroll. 1986. *Disorderly conduct: visions of gender in Victorian America*. New York: Oxford University Press.

Solomon, Barbara Miller. 1985. *In the company of educated women: A history of women and higher education in America*. New Haven: Yale University Press.

Stanton, Elizabeth Cady, Susan B. Anthony and Matilda Joslyn Gage, eds. 1887. *History of woman suffrage, volume I, 1848 – 1861*. New York: Charles Mann.

Sterling, Dorothy. 1991. *Ahead of her time: Abby Kelley and the politics of antislavery*. New York: W. W. Norton and Company.

Thatcher Ulrich, Laurel. 1991. *A midwife's tale: The life of Martha Ballard, based on her diary, 1785 – 1812.* New York: Vintage Books.

Welter, Barbara. The cult of true womanhood: 1820 – 1860. *American Quarterly* 18, no.2 (Summer 1966). http://wwjstor.org/stable/2711179 (accessed November 3, 2008).

Zabin, Serena. Women's trading networks and dangerous economies in eighteenth-century New York City. Early American Studies, 4, no. 2 (Fall 2006). http://muse.jhu.edu/journals/early_american_studies_an_interdisci plinary_journal/toc.eam4.2.html (accessed April 1, 2009).

Short Articles Concerning Nantucket History from Historic Nantucket, *a Publication of the Nantucket Historical Association*

Clarke, Joan Elrick. 1998. The Eliza Starbuck Genealogical Record. *Historic Nantucket* 47, no 1: 8 – 9.

Dixon, Alice. 1993/1994. Lydia Folger Fowler: A lesser known daughter of Nantucket. *Historic Nantucket* 42, no 4: 63 – 65.

Gessler, Christina. 2000. Researching the diary of Martha Fish: Writing a woman's life. *Historic Nantucket* 49, no 4: 15 – 17.

Haring, Jacqueline Kolle. 1992. 'Captain, the lad's a girl!' *Historic Nantucket* 40, no 4: 72 – 73.

Jenness, Amy. 2004. Azubah Cash's whaling days. *Historic Nantucket* 53, no 4: 5 – 8.

Jensen, Cecil Barron. 1997. Views from the ship *Nauticon*: One woman's journal. *Historic Nantucket* 46, no 3: 4 – 8.

McCleary, Helen Cartwright. 1929. Phebe Ann (Coffin)

Hanaford: The 100th anniversary of her birth. *Nantucket Historical Association Proceedings* XXXV.

Newell, Aimee. 2001. 'If we will but an effort make': The sewing circles of Nantucket's Congregational, Methodist, and Unitarian churches. *Historic Nantucket* 50, no 1: 10 – 13.

Stout, Kate. 1998. Who was Eliza Starbuck Barney? *Historic Nantucket* 47, no 1: 10 – 12.

Sturdevant, Lucy Huston. 1922. Two Quaker Teachers. *Proceedings of the Nantucket Historical Association, 48 – 54.*

Tetrault, Lisa M. 2002. A paper trail: Piecing together the life of Phebe Hanaford. *Historic Nantucket* 51, no 4: 6 – 9.

Tyler, Betsy. 2004. Edmund Fanning I presume; Or, how to flesh out a life through local records. Historic Nantucket 53, no 2: 11 – 15.

Weeks, Emily. 1912. Women of Nantucket. *Proceedings of the Nantucket Historical Association, Eighteenth Annual Report.*

White, Barbara. 1992. The integration of Nantucket public schools. *Historic Nantucket* 40, no 3: 59 - 62.

Short articles located in other sources at the NHA

Cohen, Judith. 1987. Nantucket's prophetess: Anna Gardner's fight for reforms. *Cape Cod Life*, Feb/Mar 46 – 49. NHA "Anna Gardner" Blue File.

Gavin, Alison M. 2008. A tale of two women: Seventeenth-century Coffin and Starbuck matriarchs. *New England Ancestors* 9, no 4: 21 – 24.

Stern, Madeleine B. 1977. Lydia Folger Fowler: First American woman professor of medicine. *New York State Journal of Medicine*. NHA "Women" Blue File.

Ucci, Diane. 1991. Whaling voyages and Quaker ideals: Creation of the Nantucket women's working force. *Nantucket Guide*. NHA "Business and Industry" Blue File.

White, Barbara. 2005. Anna Gardner: Teacher of freedmen, "a disturber of peace." Paper presented in 2005 as a James Bradford Ames Fellow.

Other Sources

Beegel, Susan Ph.D. Personal communications on sources and Nantucket women.

Karttunen, Frances Ruley Ph.D. Personal communication regarding her research on Hannah Cook Boston.

Schulte, Janet E. Ph.D. Personal communications on sources and discussions concerning women working in the nineteenth century.

Turner, Frederick Jackson. 1935. *The frontier in American history*. New York: Henry Holt and Company.

General Index

Adams, Deborah Coffin Hussey 21, 77, 78

Adultery 69

African American, also "black" 60-63, 89, 92, 94, 95, 100, 103

    Meetinghouse 89

    School 62, 92, 97

American Academy of Arts and Sciences 86

American Academy of Science 86

American Philosophical Society 86

American Revolution 30, 31, 33, 35-36, 44, 46-48, 55, 59

Association for the Advancement of Women 86, 94, 95, 98, 100

Atheneum (Nantucket) 2, 63, 93, 104

    The Strangers' Book 63

Atlantic Silk Factory 72, 73

Atlantic Straw Works, also Atlantic Straw Company 72, 73, 74

Ballard, Martha 47

Barney, Eliza Starbuck 62, 72, 76-77, 103-107

Barney, Nathaniel 103, 104

Barney, Sarah 28-29

Bible 18, 20

Boston, Absalom 61, 89

Boston, Hannah Cook 61, 89-91

"Boston Marriage" 70-71

British, also Great Britain 29, 30, 31, 32, 33, 34, 35, 36, 59, 60, 110

Cape Cod, Mass. 1, 16, 41

Centre Street, Nantucket, see also Petticoat Row 2, 75, 76, 79, 80

Chalkey, Thomas 22

Christianity, also Christian 13, 17

Coffin School 2, 71

Coffin, Anna Folger 77

Coffin, Eliza G. 6

Coffin, Kezia Folger 30-35, 37

Coleman, Priscilla 23

Congregationalists 27

Connecticut 55, 99

"Coof" 59, 64

Corporate Family Economy 9-12, 13, 14, 25, 26, 28, 35, 39, 44-45, 51, 59, 75, 81, 86

Dall, Caroline 72, 76

de Crèvecoeur, Hector St. John, also *Letters from an American Farmer* 2, 16, 26, 27, 30, 31, 34, 36, 66, 67, 68, 70

Desegregation 60

Douglass, Frederick 93, 103

Factories, also manufactories 8, 12, 43, 44, 46, 48, 49, 67, 70, 72, 74, 75

Fanning, Kezia Coffin 34

Fowler, Lorenzo 108, 110

Fowler, Lydia Folger 84, 92, 108-113

Freedmen's Aid Society 62, 94

    Bureau 62, 93

    New England Freedmen's Union Commission 62, 93

    Schools 93

Friends, see Quaker

Frontier 3, 5, 6, 8, 9-12, 14, 17, 19, 23, 25, 28, 31-35, 38-39, 40, 43, 44, 45, 47, 49, 51, 53, 59, 64-65, 75, 84, 86, 87

Fox, George 17, 20

Gardner, Anna i, 62-63, 92-97, 103

Garrison, William Lloyd 92, 93, 103

Goldenrod Literary and Debating Society for Girls 71

Hadwen, Eunice 103

Hadwen, William 104

Hanaford, Reverend Phebe Coffin i, 71, 84, 94, 98-102, 108

Harris, Elizabeth 19

Harvard College 86

He's at Homes 69-70, 71

Inquirer and Mirror 6, 73, 100

Joy, Charlotte Austin 86

King, Gertrude Mitchell 71

Lay system 65-66

Liberator, The 92

Loyalists 30, 32,

Macy, Caleb 37

Macy, Judith 37-38

Macy, Obed 37

Macy, Silvanus 38

Maine 47, 55

Mariner's Power of Attorney 57-58

Massachusetts, including Bay Colony 1, 13, 15, 19, 25, 31, 34, 46, 49, 51, 52, 60, 73, 76, 89, 94, 98, 99, 104, 108, 110

    Boston 39, 51, 76, 83

    Foxboro 73

    Gloucester 49-51, 53, 55, 76, 84

    Lowell 46

    Marblehead 49, 51-54, 55, 76, 84

    Martha's Vineyard 13, 52

    New Bedford 85, 103

    Salisbury 13

Midwife, also midwifery 47, 109, 110

Mitchell, Maria i-ii, 1, 2, 4, 5, 6, 8, 36, 63, 83, 84, 86, 87, 92, 94, 98, 100, 104, 108

Monthly Meeting 21, 23, 24, 28, 29

Mott, Lucretia Coffin i, 39, 57, 66, 70, 75, 77, 83, 84, 86, 98, 103, 108, 109

Nantucket Maria Mitchell Association i-ii, 3, 4

Nantucket Monthly Meeting 23, 24

Nantucket Straw Loan Association 73

Nantucket Straw Works, also Nantucket Straw Company 72, 73, 74

Nantucket Steamboat Company 89

National Dress Reform Association 86

"New Guinea" (Nantucket) 61-62

New England Yearly Meeting, or Yearly Meeting 21, 23, 24, 29, 35

New York 11, 15, 16, 48, 52, 54, 55, 56, 83, 94, 104, 108, 109, 110

       Oneida County 11, 14, 16, 17

       Seneca Falls 83

Nye, Mary 77, 79

Old North Wharf, Nantucket 77

Opium 67-68, 71

Peirce, Cyrus 92, 108

"Petticoat Row" on Nantucket, see also Centre Street, Nantucket 75-78, 79, 80

Philadelphia, PA 29, 35, 55, 56, 57, 94

Pleasant, Mary Ellen 63

"Private Sphere" 11, 20, 40

"Public Sphere" 8, 11, 20, 24, 39, 81

Puritan, also Puritans, also Puritanism 13, 16, 18, 19, 20, 23

Quaker, also: Quakers, Quakerism Friends, Society of Friends 1, 2, 3, 6, 9, 13, 17-21, 22, 23, 24, 25-29, 30, 31, 32, 34, 35, 38, 41, 43, 49-50, 52, 55-60, 62-64, 67-68, 70, 72, 73, 75, 81, 83, 84, 85, 86, 92, 94, 95, 98, 99, 103

Hicksite 73

Inner Light 18, 20

Quaker Meeting 19, 21, 23-25, 27, 28, 29, 34, 70, 75, 83, 94, 99

Radical Spiritualists, also radical spiritism or spiritists 22, 25

Rhode Island Yearly Meeting 23, 24, 29, 55

Richardson, John 22, 23

Ross, Eunice 62, 92

Schools, including cent, dame, African, Coffin School, private, public, "normal," schooling 2, 46, 51, 56, 57, 60-62, 70, 74, 87, 89, 92, 93, 94, 97, 98, 103, 108, 109, 110, 111,

    Female seminaries or academies 46, 70

    Women's colleges 46, 70, 86, 104

She-merchant 12-13, 22, 30, 31, 35, 85

Ships, see also whaleship, steamship 2, 31, 35, 42, 52, 55, 58, 59, 60, 61, 62, 65, 66, 67, 68, 77, 89, 91

    Catawba 114; *Island Home* 62, 89, 91; *Industry* 61, 89

Slavery, also anti-slavery 62, 73, 92, 93, 98, 103, 104

"Smashes" 70, 71

Smith, Sara Winthrop 71

"Social Sphere" 11

Sorosis 62, 86, 94, 95, 98

Stanton, Elizabeth Cady 57, 83

Starbuck, Dorcas 23

Starbuck, Jethro 23

Starbuck, Joseph 103

Starbuck, Mary Coffin, also Great Mary, Great Woman 22-25, 29, 34, 37, 50,

Starbuck, Nathaniel 22, 23

Story, Thomas 22

Suffrage 78, 87, 94, 100, 104

Swain, Harriet Myrick 58, 114

Swain, Obed 114

Trott, Anna 23

Universalist Church 98, 99

Vassar College 86, 104

Virginia 53, 94

Wampanoag 13, 16, 17, 30, 54, 61

War of 1812 59

Wesco (Nantucket) 14

Whale, also whalefishery, whaling, whaleship 2, 29, 30, 31, 34, 36, 42, 52, 54, 58, 59, 60, 61, 62, 65-66, 67, 68, 70, 72, 77, 89, 103, 115

Women's Congress 94

Women's Press Club 99

Women's Monthly Meeting 24, 28, 29, 38

Women' Rights 66, 75, 78, 83, 86, 87, 92, 94, 95, 98

Woman's Sphere 42, 44-46, 54-57, 68, 81, 100

Women's Yearly Meeting 24, 29

Wright, Martha Coffin 83, 84

Made in the USA
Middletown, DE
27 April 2017